The Shoreditch Tales

CAROLYN CLARK
& LINDA WILKINSON

front cover *Andreetti's café, Hoxton Steet, around 1910.*
back cover *Lily Yeomans and family in Shenfield Street, around 1930*

Researched & written by:
Carolyn Clark and Linda Wilkinson

Design & typography:
David Barlow

New photography & imaging:
Digital Asset Response

Copyright:
Carolyn Clark and Linda Wilkinson

Published by:
Shoreditch Trust

ISBN 978-0-9563222-1-0

Contents

Shoreditch, where's that?

Before the 1990s, most people outside the area had only a shadowy idea, if any at all, as to where Shoreditch was, and that was usually courtesy of the nursery rhyme 'Oranges and Lemons'. As for Hoxton, that was so far off the radar that the common response if you told an outsider where you came from was "Hoxton, where's that?"

Hard to believe that, today, the triangle encompassed by Great Eastern Street, Shoreditch High Street and Old Street is world renowned for artists, galleries and clubs. Where Fish and Chips ruled, you can dine on any cuisine.

There remains a certain ambivalence among the established community towards these arrivistes, who have put Shoreditch so definitively on the global map. One wonders if it's so different, though, to when Shakespeare showed up in Shoreditch and when the first theatre was built here, and, although the Pimlico pleasure gardens are a few centuries away from the all night clubs, is it so new?

Shoreditch has always been its own sweet self. From ignoring Elizabeth I when she declared that no more housing should be built, through to the dissenting religious worship which was established in Hoxton Square, and on to today, where a vast mixture of races and lifestyles live cheek by jowl, Shoreditch has always been a melting pot of ideas, ideologies and peoples. It remains a truly exciting and alive part of one of the greatest cities in the world.

left Andreetti's café, Hoxton Street, around 1910.

above Curtain Road 1897.

If some change is viewed as imposed from the outside, there is other change rooted in, and driven by, the established communities. From within, neighbourhood groups, run on a wing and a prayer for and by local people, and unsung heroes, contribute to the vitality of Shoreditch.

The area focused on in this book has, to date, felt minimal impact from the fashionable Hoxton Triangle, but that too is altering. Shoreditch is evolving all of the time, and people experience this differently. This book records the experiences and recollections of long-term Shoreditch

residents. In a changing world, these are a valuable part of the thread that links the past with the present and weaves the future.

Media hype would lead one to believe that Shoreditch has been wiped clean of its peoples, and replaced wholesale with the new. Not so; one of the most striking things about working on this book has been seeing the strength of the working class community which is still here, one that has no intention of moving on. People know one another and not just in passing. Shared memory is one of the strongest bonds and they have that in spade loads.

Hokey Pokey

It was one of the few truly hot summer days that 2008 offered to the residents of Shoreditch, and we were sitting with some of them in St Mary's Estate Hall. This is just one of several Tenant and Resident Halls which pepper the estates of the area. Estates built in the 1930s or since WWII, either because bomb damage had rendered the area uninhabitable, or as a result of 'slum clearance' when swathes of houses, some of which would today be done up and cherished, were bulldozed.

Some reported the joy of a new place you could keep clean, warm and, the icing on the cake, which had an inside loo and a bathroom. But some, uprooted from nearby houses to live in these flats, have never truly liked their newer environments, even though that newness is now over half a century old. What is missed most is the street life that came with the houses.

On one of the coldest autumn days, we sat outside Mr Samwidges café in Whitmore Road talking to the regulars about Hoxton Market as the centre of street life and mecca for all ages – a magical mix of noise and smells, full of character and opportunities.

left Kay Stone, Kathleen Doyle and Doreen Bullock from St Mary's Estate, 2009.

above Outside Mr Samwidges with the authors and, from left, Steve Hiscott, Terry Briggs and Steve Collis, 2009.

The roughness, which was a byword for Shoreditch in the early to mid-twentieth century, barely rates a mention as the café regulars talk about the past. An occasional acknowledgment that this or that street was supposedly too rough to walk down is shrugged off as of no real importance to everyday life, and it probably wasn't.

Talking to people who have lived in Shoreditch all their lives, you get a real sense of the earthy grittiness of life. Not a bland life, not an impoverished life, but one full of people, bustle and possibility. Much of that life was and is lived out on the streets, notably in the markets.

If Old Street and Kingsland Road are the arteries laid down by the Romans to take their messages of invasion and commerce throughout Britain, Hoxton Street market became the backbone that supported the local infrastructure. The place where you could be hatched, matched and dispatched; fed, clothed, watered and entertained. Schools abounded nearby, jobs were available in the light industries for which the area was known. Real poverty existed, with that no one would disagree, but in a time before welfare was state run, Shoreditch was served by its own and a few enlightened outsiders, with enough to keep body and soul together. It is the street life, though, that astounds the most. People talk about a place teeming with people day and night.

Back in the present, the group of women at St Mary's have settled into a discussion of ice cream, or rather the lack of it. Heads are being scratched to recall a shop that sold it. None comes to mind, and then arrived one of those moments which telescopes the past and present almost into one. Someone recalls a bloke who wandered around selling ices, someone else remembers half a name and suddenly there is another whole history to investigate in the guise of the 'Hokey Pokey' man, whom they all now agree used to roam the area selling ices and ice cream well into the 1950s.

Not for Shoreditch, it seems, the glories of an ice cream parlour, with sundaes, cherries on top and long metal spoons to delve into the wonders of a deep, ridged glass filled to the brim and topped with cream. No, a man with a handcart who called out "Hokey Pokey" on Sunday afternoons, breaking parents' well earned weekend naps and delighting the kids who were out playing on the streets.

His predecessors appear in Henry Mayhew's 1851 report 'London Labour and London Poor'. These vendors were new then, a curiosity which lasted well into the twentieth century. The name 'Hokey Pokey', it is thought, came from the Italian vendors' street cries as they plied their trade in ice cream. There are several suggestions as to its origin: a derivation of Hocus Pocus, a corruption of the Italian 'Ecco un poco' (Here's a little), or 'O che poco' (Oh, how little) – the last one referring to price, rather than the quantity, which gives it the most plausibility.

The vibrancy of Shoreditch far predates the mid-nineteenth century and the arrival of ice cream, however. The recollections of the people who form this living memoir stretch back over a century. Handed down through generations, told, seldom written, these are the tales which are the currency of communities the world over; the stories that until recently never appeared in history books. Every community has its own take on the past. Urban working class stories in Britain have common themes whether they come from Manchester, Swansea, Glasgow or Belfast. Yet being on the edge of what was for a long time the richest city on earth, Shoreditch is unique.

left Victorian holder for a 'penny lick' of ice cream. Hygienically replaced by the cone at a later date. following Pitfield Street in 1918.

The first suburb

The area wasn't developed until mediaeval times, with Hoxton and Haggerston appearing in the Doomsday Book of 1086 (as Hocheston and Hergotestane). Hoxton had sixteen cottages and three plough teams. 1993 excavations in Nuttall Street found a medieval oven, suggesting this was the location of the old village. Records suggest that Haggerston started off as a Roman army camp, or a place where the Saxon leader, Hergod, laid a memorial stone at an earlier date.

Shoreditch first appears in manuscripts in 1148. Theories abound on how it got its name: from the sad demise in a ditch of Jane Shore, a king's mistress, to literally a sewer ditch. A family called Soerdich had a mansion in the area about 700 years ago but there was a Dame Emma of Shordyche 100 years earlier. So, it may well stem from the Anglo Saxon name for the area: Sordig

From fields, to market gardens, to brick making, and from windmills to bowling greens, to tea houses and theatres, the Shoreditch area really took off from the 16th century. Shoreditch countryside was a favourite resort for recreation, including archery for City folk. Henry VIII gave a local archer, Barlow, the title of 'Duke of Shoreditch'. But there were already signs of tensions between the neighbours: when Shoreditch farmers tried to demarcate fields in 1516, men from the City came to tear down fences and fill in ditches so they could continue to roam free with their bows and arrows.

An Actual Survey of the Parish of St Leonard in Shoreditch, Middlesex, taken in the Year 1745, by Peter Chassereau, Surveyor. Richard Bowles, Peter Buckmaster, Church-Wardens.

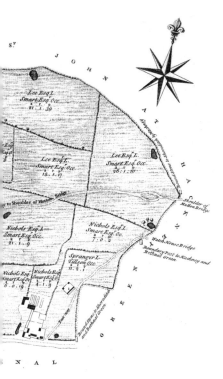

Leisure pursuits continued with theatres and tea gardens adding to the entertainment choices. This attracted the wealthy to settle, including the Portuguese ambassador and Lord Monteagle who exposed the gunpowder plot. Street names of today such as Wenlock, Pitfield, Balmes, originate from the wealthy residents from this era.

Shoreditch was lucky to escape the great fire of London in 1666, although 2000 Shoreditch residents died from the Great Plague the year before. Hoxton Square and Charles Square were created in the 1680s. Hoxton Market was built between the two Squares in 1683, but was never actually used as a market place, being already too small when completed. The street market won the popular vote, then as now.

left Chasserou's Survey of Shoreditch, 1745.

below Charles Square, about 1900.

These developments made Shoreditch one of the first London suburbs. Fine Georgian houses and terraces followed. There were also alms houses and asylums built to take the City's poor and unwell. Many of the asylums were notorious for their abusive treatment. In 1761, London's first bypass was completed. City Road was the south east extension.

Shoreditch was soon to become an inner city area as London spread and industrialisation made its mark. By 1750, the population reached an estimated 10,000, growing to 35,000 in the next 50 years and to 130,000 in 1851. On Hoxton Street, there were reputedly 449 households in the 1851 census with 1,879 residents, 40% being under 18 years of age. Overcrowded homes, often with one family per room within a tenement house, were normal. As late as 1920, a quarter of the people in Shoreditch lived two to a room. Home working for the garret master meant this was often also the workspace for sewing or furniture making, or anything else that brought food to the table. No wonder the streets were crowded.

below A Hoxton family with a visitor from the Hoxton Market Christian Mission in 1937. The small house was home to seven children and two adults.

By 1850, the once rural outpost on the edge of the City had truly disappeared. Charles Dickens often visited the area. He had Oliver Twist living in South Shoreditch and David Copperfield lodging with Mr Micawber who says: "My address, sir, is Windsor Terrace, City Road". The opening of the Regent's Canal in 1820 made timber transportation easier, and Shoreditch became the centre of the furniture industry. But there were dozens of small workshops and factories covering a host of other manufacturing and trades. Shoreditch railway station opened in 1840 where Old Street meets the Kingsland Road. Old Street Station opened much later in 1901.

Like other areas bordering the great cities of Britain, the explosion in house building and immigration was predominantly unplanned and chaotic. Whereas, most of the migrants to London at this point came from immediately neighbouring counties, this did not hold true for Hoxton Street: only 61 households came from nearby. Others came from places such as Somerset, Norfolk, Gloucestershire or Durham. A handful came from Scotland, Ireland, and Wales or from abroad. As Henry Mayhew put it in his 'Morning Chronicles' in 1851, London was 'magnificent and appalling'.

Shoreditch was now a place reminiscent of the City of London during Elizabethan times; heaving with people, many of whom were ill-fed and the majority of whom lived in inadequate and overcrowded accommodation. Clothing was hand-me-downs and footwear a luxury. Survival was the priority, but people still worked, rested and played, although rest was in short supply. Shoreditch people survived on their wits and hard graft. Shoreditch was shaped and structured by streets lined with buildings – homes and businesses – often built quickly and cheaply, side by side and packed with life.

Shoreditch people had a lot to occupy their time through the centuries: dissenters, asylums, Shakespeare, grand religious houses and the ever present proximity of the City of London, the power house that drove an empire.

We are by now at the height of Empire in the UK. The docks are importing goods from all over the world. London is growing at an ever faster rate and Shoreditch enters living memory, albeit via parents and grandparents, of people who are alive today. This is their story.

The following map of Shoreditch is reproduced from the 1893 Ordnance Survey with the kind permission of the Ordnance Survey. The white patch is where the notoriously rough area known as the Old Nichol was being demolished and replaced with the Boundary Estate.

following *OS Map of Shoreditch in 1893.*

Not a place for contemplation, or repose

Below is a first-hand description of what Hoxton Street Market was like in 1872. It is an almost complete reproduction of an article published in the Hackney & Kingsland Gazette. Hoxton High Street is synonymous with the Hoxton Street of today.

SUNDAY MORNING IN HOXTON
High Street – Special

There, around a fish stall, fifty or more persons, principally women, are congregated to examine the finney tribes upon a barrow, or make small purchases of humble luxuries for the family dinner. There again, at the greengrocer's shop, a number of others are bargaining for stale cabbages of yesterday, or enfolding in their aprons a few potatoes to eke out the scanty meal that awaits at their homes. Homes! Yes: these poor people mostly have homes, and a family that link them to their lowly dwellings stronger than any silken bond of fashionable finery. Some are looking with manifest envy at the gaudy treasures exhibited in the cheap jewellery shops; or with still greater earnest they are examining the texture of a baby's frock or a tiny pair of boots; but clearly these women are 'bent on business'; they have not left their families merely to spend an idle hour; but are seeking to purchase food or clothing, or some cheap article of household use.

left *Hoxton St, 1890.*

Then again there are the 'sellers', a group as varied still both in their aspect and sellings. Butchers with scraggy bits of meat, ornaments lying about in profusion, watercress-sellers, with baskets over-filled with the emerald dainty; dried fish merchants with plentiful supply of herrings both grey and brown, and split up haddocks in piles and layers of brown mahogany; 'purveyors' of mackerel for the most part 'of great antiquity,' whose flabby eyes and lustreless complexion bore striking evidence to the fact of lengthy absence from the sea; shrimp and winkles sellers, dealing out penn'erths of shellfish, and extolling their excellence in superlative phrases; cats' meat vendors reminding the buyer of poor puss; then there

was the clothes-line man; and the girl with wallflowers, whose perfume scented the air delightfully around her stall.

Two gentlemen were not in the mercantile department, but were of the operative class, and had established stations at different points for blacking boots, but their business did not appear to be a very flourishing condition; 'boots to be cleaned,' or those who could pay for a polish, were evidently few in Hoxton. There was one barrow with a few garden plants on it at 'a penny a root;' and a woman with toy whips of great brilliancy at the great price of one halfpenny apiece.

above Hoxton Street 1890 with the Green Man on the centre right.

The sound emanating from this heterogeneous assemblage of itinerant merchants baffles all description, the noise was incessant, and as each pair of lungs was of stentorian power, and all were hallooing at the same time and at the highest possible pressure, and as moreover, the key-notes were all differently pitched, it will be naturally concluded that there was not much musical harmony, and that Hoxton High Street on a Sunday morning was not a place one would seek for a quiet contemplation and repose. But hark! What is that? In the midst of all this turmoil and noise the sound of a single church bell of St Anne's falls upon the ear, and bid the people in the midst of all this earthly care and toil, to think of Heaven, and worship God.

Between the Pimlico Walk and the Whitmore Road, ninety-eight shops were open, while in the Walk itself, twenty seven more were devoted to various branches of business. There were whole colonies of boots, some clustering in bunches, and others wreathed like ropes of onions, outside the various establishments; while the more choice varieties of the family were kept like hot-house plants, and were seen only through glass. The bird-fancier had his feathered merchandise imprisoned in countless little cages, and were parading up and down in front thereof to catch a customer if possible. The poor little linnets looked unhappy; the woods were their home, but alas! They were mercilessly doomed to be deprived of liberty for life. Then there were the host of clothiers shops with new and second-hand garments of every description exposed for sale, some were dangling upon poles, others blocked up the windows, almost shutting out the daylight, while the shop fronts, in some instances, were so completely concealed that one might suppose that they, and not human beings; were the objects to be clad. There were hatters' shops, and toffee shops, and rag and bone establishments, butter shops and bakers' shops all open, and all plying their trades apparently regardless of the sacred nature of the day. Tobacconists were doing 'a good stroke of business,' and the barbers' shops were full.

Crockery and tin-shops, and drapery and millinery establishments were also open, and exposing their most tempting articles for sale, while overhead, at some of the latter were rows of distended crinolines hanging like hollow, headless malefactors, the sport of every passing breeze.

right Victorian houses in Ivy Street, looking towards Hoxton Street, in the 1920s.

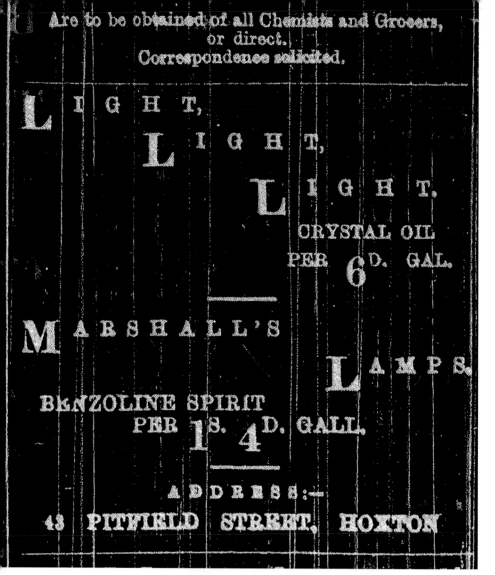

above 1864 advert from the Hackney and Kingsland Gazette.

This is an interesting article on many levels. The air of mild superiority the journalist uses is pretty typical of its time: it wasn't only the working classes who kept caged birds. Some things tally well with the descriptions given by present day residents of what the market was like, albeit a good time later. But it also misses the cheeriness of the market and the mutual support, which is another image which passes down over time.

We were baffled by crinolines wafting in the breeze. We're used to seeing crinolines in films, gracing the frames of elegant society ladies, not the likes of Hoxtonians in Victorian times. Crinolines were originally petticoats made to bulk out the skirt of a dress. This is not the place to go into depth about the origins of this peculiar garment, fascinating though it is. By the time of this article, the fashion had moved on to the bustle. It sounds as if what the market had on sale was fashion from the decade before; this ties in with a community mostly living on hand me downs and out of date fashions, but still interested in style.

There is both continuity and change in Hoxton Street traders over time. Between 1872 and 1914, number 139 remained a hat shop and number 258 stayed a jeweller. Number 5 started off as a pawnbroker's, followed by a bird dealer, then a hairdresser by 1914. Number 116 went from a launders to a furniture dealer to a toy dealer over the same timescale. Pubs are a constant, together with shops such as Andersons Bakers, Brooks Florists and Hayes & English undertakers.

inset Promotional coin for S.Homan, Shoreditch Hatter, Victorian.
below The Brooks family fruit and vegetable stall in the 1920s.

above A Shoreditch horse drawn dustcart in all its finery, ready for a day's outing.

Some people we spoke to remembered when cows and sheep were driven down Redvers Street, now Falkirk Street, from the docks to the Caledonian Cattle Market, a real link to the rural past. This spectacle continued well into the last century. Nowadays, you can still see sheep locally at Hackney City Farm in Haggerston.

The 1872 Hackney Gazette article talks about the rag and bone man, as did many of those interviewed. These urban recyclers came with a horse and cart collecting unwanted rags, used for paper or fabric manufacture, "any old iron," and bones. By the 1870s, local factories were boiling down bones for glue by the barrel load to meet the needs of the furniture industry which dominated the area. The rag and bone

man's bell and call continued to the 1970s. Local kids were always on the look out for metal, jam jars or rags. In return, they'd get a ride on the horse and cart or maybe a goldfish or piece of china. Mary Walker remembers her son disappearing out the front door with his dad's suit in the 1960s: when she challenged him, he said "I want to go on the horse". He didn't get his ride that day.

Other street vendors around for over a century were the coalman with horse and cart. Not a piece fell from his cart that wasn't put to use by local families – children would follow behind with a pram to collect the precious black stuff for their hard-pressed families. Alan Shea recalls the best time to pounce was when the cart was going round a corner.

The knife sharpener would come door to door to sharpen knives and scissors. Knives in everyday use would end up half their width but still serviceable because of regular sharpenings.

previous Hoxton Street in the 1930s.

Barrows selling food in the streets were common until about 40 years ago. Dave sold toffee apples and peanuts from a barrow all around Shoreditch. Tommy Davies sold seafood from a basket around the pubs. The chestnut seller had his brazier on wheels to roast chestnuts.

And, of course, there were the ice cream sellers, from those who sold penny licks from a tray on a strap round the neck, to the hand cart, to Mr Whippy's van complete with jingles. Alan Shea recalls Mr Montella's ice cream van in the 1960s. He'd also sell at Tottenham's Football ground on match days and was known to give local youngsters a lift home afterwards – with free ice cream to boot.

What made Hoxton Street Market so central to people's lives, however, was that all of life, and death too, was catered for on one street. Maudlin? Not really, like everything else Shoreditch did, even death had its very own style. But before that point there was a lot of life to savour.

Faggots fit for a king

This poem was written about ten years ago by Marie McCourt. Marie was born and bred in Shoreditch, living in Halstead Court in Murray Grove until her sad death in 2006. Marie was one of those Shoreditch women who are intelligent, brave, fair-minded and feisty, with a sense of community rooted in experience and a commitment to help others. She was respected by all who knew her, regardless of age, class or ethnicity. She tried her hand at many things: kendo in younger days, the local ladies' darts team later on. She worked in many places, including running a pub with her partner, Norman. She raised funds for the MacMillan Nurses and St Joseph's Hospice and was active in her Tenants' and Residents' Association. She was Vice-Chair of Shoreditch Trust. Marie had warm and abiding memories of her youth around the markets – 'the Nile' (Street) and Hoxton Street. This is her poem.

left Marie McCourt, 2005.

DO YOU REMEMBER....
Salt beef, boiled bacon, saveloys, all hot
Available at the Pork Butchers, 12 o'clock, straight from the pot
Along with pork and beef sausages, fat and thin,
Lovely tasty faggots, fit for a king?

DO YOU REMEMBER....
Pie and mash, with plenty of liquor,
Feed the family for under a nicker
Stewed eels, mash and a chunk of bread
At Fortunes, you were certainly well fed.

DO YOU REMEMBER....
Next door to Roses, especially for your Friday dinner,
George's fish and chips, with plenty of salt and vinegar
Or up near the Unicorn, there was Cohen's fish bar
Lovely grub with wallies and onions by the jar?

DO YOU REMEMBER....
Hot sarsaparilla, when it was freezing cold
From the stall, in tumblers almost too hot to hold –
And then in the summer heat
Cold drinks, at prices hard to beat?

DO YOU REMEMBER....
Murphy's finest china and hardware bargains -
How did they manage on such low profit margins?
Something for the home, gifts or wedding china
It was certainly hard to find anything finer

DO YOU REMEMBER....
Tomb, Home and Colonial, Sainsbury's and any other grocery shop
From one end of the market right up to the top?
Everything available, lovely and fresh, so you didn't have to go far
No need to travel to Dalston, Chap or Holloway by bus or car

DO YOU REMEMBER....
How we were spoilt for choice – butcher, wet fish shops, groceries, sweets and toys.
Fruit & veg, and shoes for men, women and boys?
Anything to pawn, jewellery to buy, prams and cots
From John Long's to Cohen's you could get lots

DO YOU REMEMBER....
Tom, one of my Dad's mates, with lovely meat for your cats and dogs
And all the different types of stalls for all your bits and bobs
To the mother and daughter, with fresh herbs and horseradish they grated
You could choose your fresh or raw beetroot whilst you chatted and waited

DO YOU REMEMBER....
A wander around Woolworth's or Bill's stores
Anything you need for your household chores
When people came to shop from far and wide
When plenty of shops and stalls were there 6 days a week, 9-5?

DO YOU REMEMBER....
ABC Bakers, Allwrights the butchers, Anderson's bakers (4 if I am right), the
Admiral Keppel, the Bacchus, Binysh, Bill's Stores, Browns Sweet Shop, Bloch's,
Brooks the florist, Curtis Shoe Shop, CV Shoes, Cohens, Corens, Co-op, Dog and
Cat Meat Stall, the Electricity Showroom, Fish Stalls, like Bert's, Fortunes Pie and
Mash, the Gas Showroom, George's Fish and Chips, the Green Man, Gunners,
Hairdressers, Harveys, Hayes & English, Home & Colonial, Ike's Seafood, outside
the Bacchus, Irene's, Long John, Johnson's Butchers, Kates, Kings Arms, Kitty
Mayo's, Lesley's Clothes Shop, the Launderette, Leaders Shoes, Murphy's China
and Hardware, Murphy's Fruit and Veg Stall, Nevilles the Shoe Menders, the
Opticians, Pagets, Pembertons, Philips Butchers, Pointings, Pork Butchers, Post
Office, The Queen's Head, the Roses, Sainsbury's, Swinton's and stalls galore.
Tombs Groceries, Turners Newsagents, Turner's Wet Fish, the Unicorn, Utals,
Victor Value, Woolworth's and Wooster' Fish shop?

continued overleaf

Now I'm almost pensioned
There's probably a lot I've not mentioned
Hardly any of these still exist
They are all sorely missed
From Haggerston in the East
To Windsor Terrace in the West
From along Canal Bridge in the North
To Old Street in the South

Now what have we got?
I'm sorry to say NOT A LOT!

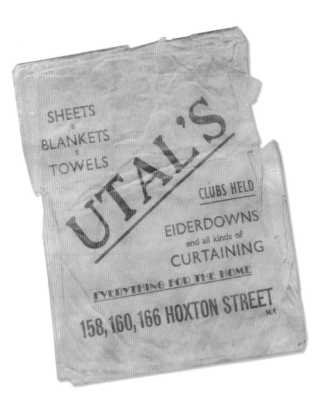

above Paper Bag from Utal's curtain shops.
right Violet and Joan, Brooks family flower shop in the 1950s.

A lifetime in a three hour walk

If the hundred and forty or so shops and stalls Marie writes about were still there, the noise alone would have told a stranger where the lifeblood of the community flowed. The market was always buzzing and full of gossip.

When Maureen Walker bought a raincoat in Hoxton Street one day, she met a friend on the way home. The news had already spread and her friend asked "What colour's your new raincoat?" That was then, but the old community has far from disappeared.

It's a weekday and the market is quiet, if not Mr Samwidges café, which is doing a roaring trade. The group we met were in their forties to fifties and were all born and raised on the streets nearby. Cars pass and people wave, or toot their horns. Others passing on foot join the group and some leave, hands are shaken and cups of tea shared. The shorthand of communication with a hand waved to signify a certain place, or a person, is well honed as befits people who know one another very well. These are people rooted in Shoreditch. Indeed, Steve Collis, one of the McLean family, says they have forty four grandchildren in the area and with such deep roots, they're here to stay.

In Mr Samwidges, we were told that in the 1950s and 1960s "you'd walk from Falkirk Street to the top of the market, and it would take three hours because you'd stop and chat when you saw someone you knew, or stop off for a drink together" and "there was a great atmosphere – we used to go down the market for hours and hours".

left Hoxton Street in 1948.

The owners live above their café and Linda, the missus, juggles work with picking her grandkids up from school. She must do an eighteen or twenty hour day. A couple of days later, walking down Hoxton Street, she recalls where the stores of yore had been.

The really busy times in the market were, of course, Friday evenings and Saturdays after the workers were paid and people were solvent for another week, or the better part of it. There was no official opening or closing time and many opened until midnight both evenings. The stalls would be lit by electric or oil lamps creating a magical atmosphere. In cold weather, they might also have braziers on the go when it was cold.

The photo below shows a typical market scene in 1948. Rationing was still in force and rabbits were an important source of meat. The man walking along the street is Mary Walker's father, Ernest Hanmer, a carpenter. Note the boots, the family say they were always polished and shiny.

below Hoxton Street in 1948.

above Hoxton Market Christian Mission Christmas Toy Service in the 1940s.

Christmas time was the high point of the year. The lights and smells encountered by those walking through the market, busier than ever, built up the excitement. On Christmas Eve, the stalls and shops stayed open until midnight – some say shops like Kitty's sold fruit and veg all night. Bakers in Anderson's Bakery would sleep on planks at the back of the shop to keep up with non-stop baking. The shop also roasted Christmas turkeys brought in by locals as they wouldn't fit into home ovens.

Mothers handled the money, as Betty Kemp recalled. She never touched the family purse until 1971 (she was 40 at this stage) when decimal coinage came in and her mother couldn't adapt to it. After an embarrassing visit to Allwrights the butchers, where her mother

misunderstood the amount charged for a cut of meat, which resulted in her storming out of the shop, Betty took over. "Mum said to me the next week, 'shall we go in there?' I said I'm not going in there again mum, you're not showing me up again."

Many people like Betty's mother went out twice a day for their shopping, some later in the day to make an evening of it. Betty continues "then at that time, my mum could get all her shopping for two pounds as well as Guinness. She used to go out 8 o'clock and get all her bread and meat before anyone else could put their hands on it. Then she'd go about 11 o'clock. Then she got everything else – Guinness, veg".

Pubs were the epicentre of the night time shop but busy during the day too. Hoxton Street had eleven pubs along its length and there were numerous others dotted around the streets. It seems that fairly astronomic amounts of booze were drunk over a weekend. During the 1950s at the Kings Arms alone, thirty six dozen bottles of Double Diamond and forty dozen of light ale were stocked on Saturday morning; the exercise was repeated for the Saturday evening and again for Sunday morning. Amongst all of the descriptions, nobody mentioned problems from drinking, although there clearly were. A rare comment was about one rather jolly woman who regularly woke Gwen Plume and her new husband up as she staggered home from the Queen's Head singing 'Red Sails in the Sunset'. This may have been the same person Joyce Howes remembers, called Martha Green. She had a fine, powerful voice which she insisted on using to boom out all the old songs when leaving the pub. This might have been appreciated at an earlier time of the evening, but not when people needed their hard-earned sleep.

left Betty Kemp, 2009.

A little of what you fancy

BY ORDER OF YOUR Local:

ADMIRAL KEPPEL	LONDON APPRENTICE
ACORN	LORD NELSON
BACCHUS	MACBETH
BARING ARMS	QUEEN'S HEAD
BEEHIVE	RED LION
BRICKLAYER'S ARMS	ROYAL STANDARD
CARPENTERS ARMS	STAG'S HEAD
CHARLIE WRIGHT'S	STURT ARMS
CROSBY HEAD	THE ONES
GEORGE & VULTURE	UNICORN
GLUE POT	VICTORY
GREEN MAN	WENLOCK ARMS
KING'S ARMS	WEYMOUTH ARMS
KING'S JOHN'S HEAD	WHITE HORSE
LION & LAMB.	WINDMILL

SHOREDITCH ALES

Children were accommodated in pub family rooms. These were frequently tiled palaces with Egyptian or other topical themes stamped on them and were away from the bar area. Either that or children stood outside with their packet of crisps and salt in a blue twist of paper, whilst parents socialised inside. Tom Carlow remembers women shelling peas in the pub for the Sunday dinner.

There were two pie and mash shops originally: Fortune's and Ford's – and now one: Cookes. Joe Cooke's grandfather opened a pie and mash shop in Sclater Street in 1862. The Cookes and Fortunes are related by marriage, and have run traditional pie and mash shops for almost 150 years. Joe Cooke carries on the family trade and opened his shop in Hoxton Street in 1987 in what was the 'Barclays Penny Bank'. It still has the strong room in the basement.

Alan Shea says "the pie and mash shops were banged out to the rafters on a Saturday... it was a meeting point for traders and shoppers". During the week, school children were big users at lunch times. In the early days, you could get a penny pie and halfpenny of mash. Mash and liquor cost 6d or one shilling with a pie in the 1960s. You could have as much salt as you wanted, but the pepper pot was on a string so it didn't get nicked. Now it's £4 for the full monty, or £1 for a pensioners' meal – and it's still made from scratch every day in the same way it's always been.

Fortune's pie and mash shop was on the same site opposite Hoxton Hall for about 100 years. Mick and Bob Walker both worked there, Mick from 1969 and Bob, starting off as a Saturday boy, from 1970 until 1980, when the shop closed. The original cast iron range fired with coke was still in use, only later changed to oil. In summer, especially the scorcher of 1976, Bob says it was baking down there – in more ways than one.

above Fortune's pie and mash shop in 1985.

Pie and mash was a poor man's meal, but still used quality products. All the meat came fresh from Harry Allwright's and the potatoes came from the market. Every two weeks, Mick or Bob recalled "driving down to Dorset with the governor to get the eels from Don the fisherman. He got them out of the River Piddle". Nowadays, Joe Cooke gets his eels from the Isle of Sheppey or Billingsgate.

The kitchens were especially busy on Friday and Saturday, with continual queues from 10 to 3 or 4pm, "except on Cup Final days" Bob adds. Besides celebrities from Hoxton Hall like Tommy Steele, customers were mainly locals. But Mick once served an American who asked "Is it true you pour alcohol on your pies?" So, in his honour, here's the method for making naturally green liquor, courtesy of Mick:

Mix flour and water into a batter
Boil water and add to batter
Add fresh parsley, freshly minced
Add salt
Stir

Joe Cooke considers Maris Piper the best potato and reports his shop gets through one and a half tons of fresh parsley a year. Joe also has Americans in the shop: a recent group asked if he had many visitors from abroad. Joe affirmed he did and listed all the nationalities he has in, then listing the religions – Roman Catholics, Anglicans, Muslims, Hindus, Jews, the lot. They then asked "and Mormons?". It turned out they were Mormons on a trip from Utah.

Fish and chips were more of a treat as they cost one shilling and sixpence in the 1960s. However, Corran's sold yesterday's chips, refried, cheap. Nothing was wasted. Alan Shea recalls with relish paying a few pence for a bag of the small crispy bits of batter which fell off the fish during frying. People told of wandering with their mates and getting half a loaf of bread from Anderson's, pulling out the middle, filling it with yesterday's chips from Corran's and sharing it. Or maybe a penny's worth of yesterday's cakes was what they fancied, all washed down with hot or cold sarsaparilla depending on the time of year. Then they'd hang around their favourite stall or shop and natter.

above Robbo in 1980.

The market was a source of endless entertainment where you could "step outside and get everything on your doorstep". Here's a run through of the traders people mentioned from the last fifty years.

'Twonose' pulled out the stalls: his nickname reflected the large growth on his nose. Some stallholders were real characters who put on a show, calling out to attract customers. The biscuit man's catchphrase was "Watch out, big brother's watching you". At Mr Samwidges, they talked about Ginger Loo or Toodaloo. Steve Hiscott says "He was a real life Del Boy. He never had a pitch but would turn up from nowhere with a cardboard box selling things like crackers. He'd call out 'any old bill around? I've got some bent goods here', even though they were straight as a die."

Traders used to specialise more and could well be known by both their name and their product: Mick the biscuit man, the fish man, the key man, the pickles man. Beetroot Rose boiled her beetroot in Ivy Street and sold it on Hoxton Street "hot and sweet". Nowadays, there's less specialism: no watercress sellers, although fruit and veg abound. Robbo ran his pickles stall for about 50 years from the turn of the 20th century. He was good at calming people down when they themselves got into a pickle, too. At one meeting he was at, aged over eighty, there was a dispute brewing. The antagonists collapsed in laughter when he announced sagely "You can't make an omelette without breaking eggs".

Natty Bloch's Grocers at 151 Hoxton Street was used in the film about the Krays. Edie Murphy says "It was so packed with stuff – barrels of smoked herring, great bowls of pickles and rollmops – there was hardly any room for customers. It was always old-fashioned, about 30 years in the past". Terry Briggs remembered "he could add up faster than any calculator". Blochs would stand outside and shout to customers "I've got something for you" but it was usually only broken biscuits sold from barrels. The Mr Samwidges group joked "We never knew what a whole biscuit looked like when we were young". Edie Murphy remembers, as a child, calling into Bloch's "Got any broken biscuits?" and, when the reply was yes, calling back "then mend them" before running off. Bloch's gave as good as he got by all accounts and any child caught nicking got 'a clip round the ear'.

above Sainsbury's. in Hoxton Street around 1900.

right Linda Anderson serving tea in Anderson's Bakery, 2009.

Home and Colonial sold all sorts of groceries. If they had stock that had been hanging around for too long (there were no sell by dates then), such as a jar of jam, they'd give it away to customers. As a major shopping street, Hoxton attracted chain stores early on. From 1905 to 1919 there was a Sainsbury's near where the pie and mash shop is now. It was a tiny shop compared to current supermarkets, by all accounts. The biggest shop in Hoxton Street in living memory was the Co-op, where Iceland is now. There was also a Woolworths on the current Peacocks site. Mick Walker once found £10 in £1 notes on the floor in Woolworths. He picked them up and handed them in. It was never claimed, so after three weeks, it was his. Alan Shea recalls many local kids ended up with Dunlop Green Flash shoes or plimsolls, as that's what Woolies sold, so "you always knew where their mums shopped".

above Ron's stall sign by Rob and Roberta Smith on the Regent's Canal.

Fruit and vegetables came from many stalls, as now. Kitty Mayo had a shop and a stall, the stall was then run by her son, Nicky and his wife Eve. Every Christmas, Kitty used to make up about 150 fruit baskets to give to local pensioners. Her's was one of the 'Hole in the Wall' shops which were opened fronted, and locked up with a shutter.

There's always been a selection of bakers. Most people have a memory of Andersons, whether it was going there at 5.30 in the morning to buy hot cross buns at Easter or, if you had the money, getting a family selection of cakes filling two carrier bags for two bob.

One of the big gaps in Hoxton market today is a fishmonger's. There were at least three wet fish sellers – 'fish on a marble slab and live eels all wriggling'. Burdett's, the kipper house, was on the corner of Purcell Street. Turner's 'smoked specialists' was close to where the library now is. Ron's shellfish stall kept the tradition alive until this year. Ron's signs, immortalised by Rob and Roberta Smith, adorned Art on the Underground posters across London in 2006. There are also giant versions of these, and other market shop signs, around Shoreditch and along the Canal.

There was no shortage of butchers. Hedges German butchers at the top of Falkirk Street sold faggots and pigs trotters. There was also West's and a Dewhurst. G&M specialised in saveloys and pease pudding, called the In and Out butchers as it was open fronted.

The butcher's shop people remember most is Harry Allwright. Betty says "He (Allwright) was very good to the old girls, he gave money to their clubs, he used to take them out on a trip. They didn't care what they said to him". George Turnell was born in Ivy Street and was a butcher most of his life. He worked for the Allwright family in their Hoxton Street shop for about 40 years from the 1930s. He was interviewed in 1984. George said that at one time there were 84 different meat shops and stalls in the market. The Allwrights had been there for over 100 years. He loved the atmosphere in the market and seeing the regulars. George recalled two 'Iron Cows' in Hoxton. These were large tanks where punters put in a penny, pulled a handle and got a pint of milk. One was in Hoxton Street before the roundabout and the other in Great James Street, now Purcell Street.

below George Turnell in Harry Allwright's butcher shop, 1940's.

Norma Edwards remembers Old Tom's stall with its sign 'Horse meat for cats and dogs only'. Her aunt would buy meat there for her dog Bruno. She was always saying "I don't know where Bruno is". One day, Tom asked her if she'd been training her dog, because he used to arrive at the stall every morning, as Tom was setting up. Bruno would wait for scraps as Tom chopped up the meat and "once he'd had his fill, woof woof and off he'd go". This was news to Norma's aunt, who was also feeding him every day.

There were dairies dotted around Shoreditch, such as Birds, run by Bill Bradbury. In the 1970s, cows were kept in the small yard next to Brooks florists. Harry Allwright's housekeeper would milk them. The Royal Eagles Dairy in Nile Street also had its own cows. D. Evans, the Fanshaw Street Dairy, advertised 'Day and Night Automatic Milk Supply' – probably from one of the iron cows George refers to.

Established 100 Years

D. EVANS

DAIRYMAN and Provision Merchant

NOTED FOR PURITY AND QUALITY

Dairy Farmer and dealer in all kinds of Dairy produce. New laid and Welsh Eggs. Fresh Dorset and Devonshire Butter. Milk delivered twice daily. Nursery Milk in sealed Bottles.

DAY AND NIGHT AUTOMATIC MILK SUPPLY

FANSHAW DAIRY

2 FANSHAW STREET, LONDON, N. 1
(Opposite Hoxton Church)

above 1930 advert for a local dairy.
left Norma Edwards, 2009.

above 1930 advert for a Haggerston dairiy.

Sweets came up in almost all our discussions: people could play for England in remembering sweets of the past. As Norma Edwards says: "It's a wonder children have any teeth left". Browns sweet shop sold ice cream from its front window into the street. Pembertons – 'Pems' – sweetshop still had the Victorian feel well into the post-war period: lots of glass cases and jars of sweets. "6d a week pocket money (in the later sixties/early seventies) would soon go on sweets". Meadows sweet stall at the top of Ivy Walk sold boiled sweets: bulls' eyes, aniseed twists, sherbet lemons, acid drops, sour apple and rhubarb and custard to name but a few. Tillsons sold newspapers, sweets and toys – it was where Mick Walker got his Scalextric at Christmas.

One of the most famous toy shops in London graced Hoxton Street until it was destroyed in the Second World War. Pollocks, based in a small rather dingy shop near the Britannia Music Hall, specialised in toy theatres and model stages. These were made from cardboard and sold for 'a penny plain and tuppence coloured'. The novelist, Robert Louis Stevenson, visited the shop and had his top hat knocked off by the toy theatres hanging from the ceiling inside.

Shoe shops included Clarks, Curtess and Vanners – the latter ran by a man who fascinated the kids with his 'big fat, curly moustache'. There were lots of clothes shops such as Kays and Basners. Levy's in Purcell Street sold school uniforms and Cohen's sold workwear such as overalls and carpenters' aprons. Lots of people spoke about Beanishes, the haberdashers, because the money was put into suction tubes and transported around the shop to where Mr Beanish sat in his glass box, stoically counting his takings. The air was filled with a whooshing sound as the speeding caskets flew around.

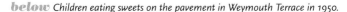
below Children eating sweets on the pavement in Weymouth Terrace in 1950.

Hairdressers and barbers feature now in Hoxton. The family lived above the shop at Harry Bratter in Falkirk Street, where "you could go for a haircut and a game of cards". Maurice Lautman, a barber for over 40 years who lived in New North Road, contributed to a book with jokes and anecdotes in the 1980s called 'Will there be anything else, sir?' One example from the book is 'My son's a famous surgeon. He's a genius. If you're at death's door, he'll pull you through'.

Casual traders enlivened the market scene and are a sad loss with the new licensing arrangements. One time, a casual turned up with boxes and boxes of handles from every decade from the 1930s to the 1980s. He tipped them out all over the pavement, looking up at passers-by with a wry smile, declaring "presentation is everything".

right Mark Brooks, 2009.
below Brooks florists decorated for the 1936 Coronation.

Brooks the florist is one of the longest established shops. Mark Brooks is often to be seen working outside his shop making the most astonishing objects. To call them wreaths is far from accurate. He's made "just about everything from bulldogs, through to angels, the lot". You name it, he and his family have done it.

Mark is a great local historian and raconteur of all things Shoreditch and beyond. He has that rare talent when he talks, of taking you back to places. You can almost smell the horses he describes and hear the sizzle of irons as they plunge into beer.

Mark lives in the flat that he created for himself behind the Florist shop, which the family still owns. The shop itself is very much like it would have been 90 years ago when it first opened, with scrubbed untreated floorboards and the glorious smell from the ferns and greenery used in the elaborate craft he and his family have perfected in 90 years in business. Mark is an affable and entertaining host, but above all he cares. Cares for the market, cares for his profession and cares for his area. He was born in 1950, but his recollections through the people he met go back to the 1880s, and he knew a lot of people.

"As a young child I used to go round Hobbs Place, it's built on now but it used to be stables. My grandfather used to be around there and I can remember going to see him." One Christmas "when I was about six, my grandfather took me there to this wooden barn with the hay above us; we climbed up into the hay. Nelly was downstairs, she was a black and white Shire horse. Behind the hay was this orange car. It was a really vivid memory, this car and him pulling it out for me. Magic."

"Then I remember the men in the Public Bar, because my mother's father had the Kings Arms pub on the corner. The stables were behind it and there was some houses mixed in with the stables. Then there were little shops coming towards St Leonards Hospital. You can see where houses used to rest up against St Anne's Church opposite. There used to be a nail shop and ironmongers to do with the stables. I remember too the men that took the iron."

right *Three likely lads outside the Kings Arms in the 1920s.*
The glazed tiles, currently painted over, are green.

Mark goes on to remember the Public Bar of the Kings Arms, in the winter of 1954 or so. Mark takes a drag on a slender roll-your-own cigarette and talks about the men, lined up on benches with their drinks, spittoons on the floor, and one man in particular.

"One chap there had elephantiasis bollocks and he used to wear a skirt. Couldn't get trousers over them, no way poor sod. Anyhow, see in winter they needed an extra bit of a fillip, keep them going. In the Kings Arms in the fireplace there were 30-40 razor sharp irons. Honed as sharp, as sharp could be. The men'd heat them til they were white hot and then put an iron in a pint of bitter, right in the centre. It steamed and smelt and then the iron floated to the top and they drank it."

He went on; "When I was a child, people were walking around with one arm or leg, having lost one in the First or Second World Wars. You always had war looking at you all the time. A bloke who lost his arm worked at Murphy's and he used to put goods under his stump to wrap them up." Murphy's was referred to by many people as where you could buy china and crockery, and rarely was a piece broken. People would buy gifts there.

Several people interviewed also remembered a sweetshop in Whitmore Road run by a man called One Arm Jack as he had lost an arm in the war. He had rows of sweet jars on tall shelves. He had to get a ladder to get one down. Kids would inevitably ask for sweets from the top shelf!

In 1982, Hoxton Street was designated a Conservation Area. The bulk of buildings from old Hoxton are there, as you can see if you look above the shop fronts. They show that Hoxton Street is essentially a village street, with buildings of all periods. These range from a five hundred year old house to St Leonards, built in 1863 as a workhouse in an Italian style, to the post-war developments where bombs had hit. Two of the finest early Georgian houses in London are next to Queen Mary's Hostel (now Hoxton Works), itself a good Tudor revival of the 1920s. These were houses for prosperous merchants. Until mid Victorian times Hoxton Street was a residential street.

left Hoxton Street market in 2007. following Interior of a Hoxton Street home, 1959. No doubt, some of the contents were purchased in Hoxton Market.

Pawn shops and tally men

Poverty and all it brings is no stranger to Shoreditch. Most of those we spoke to recalled some experience of the hard end of life. Marje Proops became a Fleet Street editor and famous agony aunt. She started life in Shoreditch – Shepherdess Walk, then Kingsland Road. She wrote "There were plenty of problems around in my childhood and youth and I know there are still plenty today". And she wasn't wrong.

Overcrowding was, and is, a big issue. In 1901, there was an average twenty four children in every Shoreditch house. A 1928 House of Commons report on housing conditions in Shoreditch recorded 'a man, wife and three boys aged 13 years, 9 years and 7 years live in one room. There is only one bed and there is only room for one. The father and boys have to go to bed first, and the mother and daughter undress behind a curtain. The mother then shares the family bed and the daughter sleeps on some chairs... the room was extremely clean and orderly when visited'. Another house in Baches Street had two rooms for a family of eight, so crowded the table had to be moved out of the window at night to make room for sleeping space. The place was impossible to keep clean and tidy and the oldest daughter, who earned twenty two shillings and sixpence a week working at the ABC bakery, was 'very much ashamed of the house and cannot bring her friends there.'

left *Wood seller in Essex Street plying her meagre trade in 1929, with the Liberal parliamentary candidate (who lost).*

above Illustration of inside a Shoreditch House in 1919
where two families comprising eleven people shared one room.

Terry Briggs, as a young lad in the 1950s, lived with his family in two rooms, sharing a cooker in the hall with the other tenants. Chatham Avenue, which is where the Blue Hut Youth Centre is now, was a tenement building. Mary Walker raised her family there in two rooms. There were two toilets down the stairs for the whole block and a sink on the landing with one cold tap serving four flats. Things improved when they moved to Phillipp Street. The flat had a kitchen which contained both the copper to wash clothes and the bath, which had a wooden cover.

The worst housing conditions, before the Luftwaffe and slum clearance made their mark, were found around Nile Street, Essex Street and Wilmer Gardens. Tom Carlow described Wilmer Gardens when he was young as "almost a shanty town".

Some of the old houses would be done up today as choice family homes, but at the time it was hard work to keep them clean and pest free. Those who moved into new flats may have felt the loss of the street life, but many welcomed the cleaner, brighter homes with an inside bathroom and toilet. Nickie Lodge lived with her husband and young child in one room in Haggerston after both did service in the war. She says: "In the army, we were promised homes fit for kings and queens, but it didn't happen." She had to go in front of a board at Shoreditch Town Hall to get a new flat and was offered a one bedroom flat in Bracklyn Court. She moved into the block on the day it opened in 1960. She was told her child had to be aged ten or more for the family to get a two bedroom flat. Nickie says of her new flat: "It was heaven... to have a bathroom and your own front door."

above Nickie Lodge celebrating the 2002 Golden Jubilee in Hoxton Street.

The pride that is taken in many Shoreditch homes today is re-enforced by memories of the conditions that most faced. Maureen Walker recalls her mother's efforts, involving creosote at first and then DDT, to keep their rooms bug free. It was always an uphill struggle as the bugs got into the fabric of the old tenement houses with their crumbling plaster and worn out wood. Before she was allowed to move into her new flat, all Nickie Lodge's furniture had to be put in a big room overnight to be fumigated.

The streets and open air were a refuge, a playground, and a place to socialise, share problems and news, make contacts, get work, and have fun. Community had a strong hold and certain myths hold true, like keys on string and open doors. Almost everyone born in the early to mid 20th century commented on the fact that, indeed, keys did hang on pieces of string behind letterboxes. And doors were left unlocked – in houses containing 4 or 5 families and kids running in and out all day, locked doors never stayed so for long. And besides, there was little to steal.

Tom Carlow recalls that lots of the houses were safe. "If you needed help, the neighbours would come to your aid. Opposite my house (in Hows Street) was Dickenson's the wheelwrights. There were two men there, one fat and one thin. We called them Laurel and Hardy. If my mum was out when I came back from school, they'd take me over there. If I so much as fell over anywhere in the street, mum would know about it."

Gwen Plume is 81 years old and has lived in Shoreditch since she was two. She recalls, "People were jolly, we knew one another and we could talk together. We felt like one big, happy family. You could knock on someone's door if you were in trouble. If they left their door open by accident you told them. Otherwise you could just walk in and out, you'd go into a person's house, you'd never dream of looking around or touching anything, you'd have a chat and out you'd come."

Nickie Lodge used to work at St John's School. The parents and children she met there still greet her many years after she left the job. In the days when she had a young family, Nickie was close friends with a neighbour and they had an arrangement: "No one had washing machines then, just little gas burners under the copper. On Monday, I did the washing and my neighbour took the baby, and on Tuesday, she'd do the ironing while I looked after the children."

right Gwen Plume, 2009.

Mary Tagoe moved to Stanway Street in 1979 and felt at home from the start. She says people were so friendly. Now she and her daughters, who grew up in the area, do not want to live anywhere else. She says "It is quiet here. There is togetherness, people still say hello. You can tell people who don't live here from the way they behave. I just saw a lady from the school my kids went to for the first time in years, and we greeted each other."

The community helped itself, making sure a little went a long way. Families and neighbours would help out where they could. Mary Walker's neighbour worked in one of the many timber yards. He'd bring home sacks of wood off-cuts for them to use as fuel. The problem was, the kids saw these as great toys and would tip the sack out. Her son, Alan, then thought the sack of coal would also be good to play with, and Mary just stopped him tipping that out too.

above Lads near Hoxton Market with a cart, 1930s.
right Mary Tagoe, 2009.

Not everyone had such a ready supply of fuel. Edie Murphy remembers with a shiver being sent out in the middle of a wet winter to try and find some coke for the family when she was young. It meant going over to Haggerston where there was a large depot serving the gas works. Edie's only shoes were plimsoles with cardboard covering the holes in the soles.

Recycling was also part of getting by. Parents made toys and kids made scooters and go-carts out of pieces of old wood. They'd take them round the streets and pick up any metal, papers, magazines or beer bottles. Towards Haggerston, they'd take them to a taxi workshop in Geffrye Street which would weigh the gear and pay. There were rag and scrap metal merchants all over the place: in Poole Street, New North Road, Coronet Street and Queensbridge Road among others. Empty beer bottles were worth a penny and later tuppence each, so these were prized items gathered after any

above Cohen's Pawn Shop, corner of Hoxton Street and Shenfield Street, 1956.

party or event. But the publicans had to be quick when taking a new delivery: if the empties were left on the pavement, they wouldn't stay in the crates for long as passing children were quick on the uptake.

Maureen Walker described second hand shops as "a life saver". Shoreditch had a wealth of these. Up to about 10 years ago, the market had second-hand stalls recycling quality as well as more common gear, such as Old Annie's. Crispin's junk yard, which started on the corner of Calvert Avenue before moving to the top of Hoxton market, was like a car boot sale. You could get everything there. Mick Walker remembers buying a Beatles style jacket for 2d (old pennies) in the 1970s. He and Bob also got a marble clock for their mother from one of the other second hand stalls for two shillings. Although high rents forced Norma Edwards out of her second hand and antiques shop – Olde Hoxton Curios – a couple of years ago, there's still a second-hand stall or two on Saturdays. Second hand clothing (fashionably called vintage) shops are now cropping up in the southern end of Shoreditch.

Pawnshops had a key role in the local economic cycle. Two pawn shops are recalled by many: Cohen's and John Long's, also called 'Long and Doubtees'. People appreciated the service they offered. "They helped a lot of people", Maureen Walker continues, "the pawn shops, what magical places they were. If we were short of money my mother used to say to me, she had this beautiful diamond ring, 'I think I'll pawn my ring'. The pawn shops always had a very narrow passage, I often wondered why? Maybe it was because people couldn't run out or rush at them. There was always a long bit between the pledged and redeemed departments. Mother used to panic if she forgot to go and pay the interest on it. John Long's was the main pawn brokers. People bought a lot of their stuff there. Buying unredeemed jewellery was good because after the war the government slapped purchase tax on jewellery. Anyone with a brain would go and buy the unredeemed goods."

George Turnell learnt this ditty from his parents:

Oh Mr Landlord,
I've got no rent for you,
My fire's gone out,
Mum's gone too,
Mother's gone to the Pawn Shop
to pawn the lodger's clothes,
My father's getting his nose red
In the pub across the road.

And besides the pawn shops, there was the tally man. People borrowed from the tally man to get things out of pawn. When the tally man came round the next week to collect, many would be out or they'd hide. Edie Murphy remembers a neighbour, Nelly Dove, who looked out of her window and saw the tally man closing in. With no time to move away from the window and hide, she "froze. chin resting on the shelves, pretending to be a statue".

This was a regular pattern of life for families trying to make ends meet: people took clothes, including school uniforms, jewellery and even bedding to pawn on Monday to get money to last the week,

right Edie Murphy, 2009.

Poor children waiting for free din

r *anything else* to do these children goo

then get them out on Friday when the pay packet arrived or the tally man called. In between, there was 'on the Book' or tick. Bloch's the grocer allowed people to buy on tick, keeping an account of how much was owed in a book. The sanction for not paying seemed to be to stop giving them tick, and to tell others about an unpaid debt. Edie pointed out, however, that telling someone that so and so was in debt didn't hold much weight as "so were a lot of people".

For those with nothing to pawn, there were the Missions. The Hoxton Market Christian Mission is the most famous and best

above *Newspaper cutting from 1929 of the daily queues outside Daddy Burtt's.*

will be welcome.

loved. It's known to everyone we spoke to as Daddy Burtt's, after its slogan 'Daddy Burtt's for Dinner'. The founder was John Burtt, later joined by his brother Lewis. They had been rescued from the streets themselves and had been educated at a ragged school. John Burtt was disabled at the age of eight by his work as a milk boy – long hours carrying the heavy yoke and pails caused a weakness in his ankles. He wanted to give children and their parents the chance he had, initially through a ragged school and later through the Hoxton Market Christian Mission. It was he and his brother's understanding and empathy, grounded in experience and reality, which earned such respect.

above Bread distribution at Daddy Burtts in the 1950s.

Daddy Burtt's was open seven days a week from 9am to 10pm, relying heavily on volunteers. This was industrial strength philanthropy needed to tackle industrial strength poverty when the welfare state was still a gleam in the father's eye.

The Mission's record of activity in a sample year in the 1920s is impressive. Two staff, receiving modest payment, and a hundred volunteers delivered the following:

- *270,460 free meals given to poor children*
- *50,972 new and used garments distributed to poor people*
- *1,789 new or repaired boots and shoes distributed*
- *662 children sent to the country or seaside or to convalescent homes for two weeks*
- *9885 children given an outing, usually to Epping Forest*
- *842 joints of meat, 1305 cwts of coal, 15,121 loaves, 8515 parcels of groceries value two shillings and downwards, 70 new blankets distributed*
- *823 hospital, surgical aid and convalescent home letters were sent*
- *On Christmas Eve, 1,121 substantial parcels of Christmas cheer distributed including coal, to poor families*
- *10,122 children made happy at special Christmas festivities*
- *8 orphan children placed in orphanages*
- *Three clinics run for poor mothers*
- *Children gathered from the streets to play inside during the cold months*

HIS AWFUL
CTURE IS
E RESULT
ONE DAYS
OOTING

AT THE
HOXTON
MARKET
MISSION&
RAGGED SCHOOL

IT REPRESENTS 90 POOR CHILDREN REBOOTED

above Advertising for donations.

The Burtts believed in, and encouraged, self-help. They taught people to mend their own boots and shoes, supplying the leather. When they were beyond repair, people got new ones. Maureen Walker recalls: "This was the good thing about Daddy Burtt's. He would not give you a new pair of boots until you gave a pair in. Theory being you just didn't hand people a pair of boots because people would just go off and sell them." Maureen and her peers have more than a passing respect for Daddy Burtt's. The local feeling seems to be that a statue, or something significant, should be erected in honour of the service done to locals by the brothers and their work.

Daddy Burtt's was only closed in the 1980s, long after the Burtts died. The building now houses the Real Greek Restaurant. What the brothers would have made of this irony would be interesting to know.

next Charles Booth's Descriptive Map of London Poverty 1889.

Lowest class.   Vicious, semi-criminal.

Very poor, casual.   Chronic want.

Poor.   18s. to 21s. a week for a moderate family.

Mixed.   Some comfortable, others poor.

Fairly comfortable.   Good ordinary earnings.

Well-to-do.   Middle class.

Upper-middle and Upper classes.
        Wealthy.

The Dust Destructor

No Shoreditch story is complete without paying tribute to the Shoreditch pioneers who broke the mould. The Shoreditch Vestry, followed by the Metropolitan Borough of Shoreditch in 1900, covered an area which was overwhelmingly poor, with very little open space and enduring housing, health and literacy problems. The people who ran these bodies were often local people themselves and they made Shoreditch a beacon for home-grown innovation.

Much has been written on how the Borough got its 'More Light, More Power' motto, adopted in 1897. In essence, it burnt waste in a 'Dust Destructor' to generate heat to supply cheap electricity to local residents. It was the first district in England to do so. In 1926, the council initiated a scheme to install electric lighting in private houses and tenements. In the late 1920s, the Borough built a new, modern electricity showroom at the Old Street end of Hoxton Street. This proudly displayed 'the very latest devices for the adaptation of electricity to lighting, heating, cooking, ventilation and other purposes'. The building still stands.

Public baths, heated by the generating station, and a public library were developed as part of the power station complex on an old ironworks site. The baths were destroyed by bombing, but the buildings which housed the 'Shoreditch Borough Refuse Destructor

above Shoreditch Council's Electricity Showrooms in 1929.

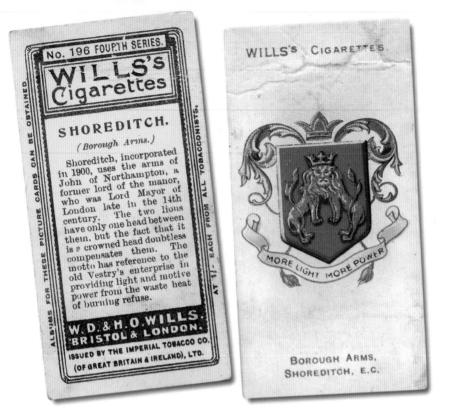

name="img_1" content="Left card — Wills's Cigarettes:

No. 196 FOURTH SERIES.

WILL'S'S
Cigarettes

SHOREDITCH.
(Borough Arms.)

Shoreditch, incorporated in 1900, uses the arms of John of Northampton, a former lord of the manor, who was Lord Mayor of London late in the 14th century. The two lions have only one head between them, but the fact that it is a crowned head doubtless compensates them. The motto has reference to the old Vestry's enterprise in providing light and motive power from the waste heat of burning refuse.

W. D. & H. O. WILLS.
BRISTOL & LONDON.
ISSUED BY THE IMPERIAL TOBACCO CO.
(OF GREAT BRITAIN & IRELAND), LTD.

ALBUMS FOR THESE PICTURE CARDS CAN BE OBTAINED.
AT 1/- EACH FROM ALL TOBACCONISTS.

Right card: WILL'S'S CIGARETTES — coat of arms with motto MORE LIGHT MORE POWER — BOROUGH ARMS, SHOREDITCH, E.C." />

above Cigarette card from the Wills London Boroughs series featuring the Shoreditch Borough Arms.

and Generating Station' in Hoxton Market and the library in Pitfield Street remain. You can see the glazed tiles used inside the baths on an end wall, at the side of the old generating station. 'E PULVERE LUX ET VIS' (from dust, light and power) stands above the entrance of the power station, which is now Circus Space. Pitfield Library is converted to flats and a theatre space.

Housing has always been a central issue locally. The London Borough of Shoreditch was the first local authority, other than the London County Council, to build a municipal housing scheme in 1899. This addressed the 'closely packed, defectively constructed and worn out dwellings' condemned by the Shoreditch Medical Officer of Health in 1890. Thirty six tenements of two rooms each, sixty three of three rooms and eight of four rooms were built in Moira Place and Plumbers Place (near Vestry Street). Each was self-contained, with running water, an inside toilet and electric lighting.

This was the first of many such schemes to improve housing conditions, some more successful than others. The Prince of Wales attended the opening of Windsor House in Shepherdess Walk in 1927. On meeting the Mayor of Shoreditch, the Prince asked his occupation. "Cabinet-maker" came the proud reply, adding "Shoreditch is the home of the cabinet-making industry". The Prince queried whether this local man, with a full time job in a manual trade, could find time to be Mayor. There is no record of the reply, but it was certain to have been polite.

below Promoting Shoreditch Electricity around 1925.

Shoreditch opened its first public library in 1893 in the former offices of the Independent Gas Company in Kingsland Road, just before the canal. The building is listed, but is now flats. Shoreditch was also the first London borough to put 'Wireless' in its libraries in the 1920s when few people locally could afford a radio of their own.

Shoreditch was a model borough in its provision of holistic maternity and child welfare services. The first centre opened in 1915, but this was replaced with the new Model Maternity and Child Welfare Centre in Kingsland Road in 1923. This included a dining

area, providing meals for nursing and expectant mothers, wards for sick children and for mothers and infants. Ante-natal, breast feeding and sunlight clinics were held there as well as in other parts of the Borough. The progressive policies included the provision of family planning advice before this was widely available.

above The Passmore Edwards Free Library, Kingsland Road around 1900.

The Sun Babies Day Nursery, just by the Rosemary Branch Bridge, was 'the biggest in the kingdom' according to a news report of its opening in 1927. There were a hundred places and the emphasis was on light and air for healthy babies. At the opening ceremony, Princess Mary, 'gowned in blue', 'on her tour of the open-air rooms was delighted with the appearance of the children' who were 'having simple Montessori instruction'.

Shoreditch was the first local authority in London to introduce municipal barrows. The lot of the costermonger (stall holder) was a hard one, and this move was a great help. A local Justice of the Peace, William Orsman (hence Orsman Road), spurred by an act of injustice against costers, developed Costers Hall in Hoxton Street to help those who worked the market. His funeral in 1923 was attended by many costers, who left their barrows to attend, a sure mark of respect.

A less heralded cause for local pride is the Shoreditch Water Closet. This was the first in the country not to be boxed in, permitting easy cleaning. It was invented in 1874 by Shoreditch's Chief Sanitary Inspector.

It didn't end there. Rose Heatley, a local resident, writes: "In 1902, J. Ruth Dixon, Engineer and Surveyor in Shoreditch, described five underground facilities he had built in this 'busy and progressive district'. He comments that women's needs had been 'hardly recognised hitherto, as evidenced by their reticence when provision was first made for them', but that women's sections were now being used as much by women as men... Charges were: use of WC, one penny; wash and brush-up, two pence; dressing room, six pence; urinettes, a halfpenny; urinal, free. Opening hours were from 6am to midnight and from 7am to 11pm on Sundays and bank holidays. Attendants could allow 'obviously poor people who express an inability to pay' to use a specially set-aside WC for free. Mr Dixon reported that most toilets were 'fairly remunerative'; some sanitary ware providers had seen the commercial opportunity, constructed and operated their own public toilets, paying local authorities for the privilege, but he disapproved. In his view they should be seen primarily as conveniences for the public, not profit-earning institutions."

Unfortunately, this tradition did not survive into the later 20th century. There was no public toilet in Hoxton Street for many years. A campaign in the 1980s to put public loos into Stanway Street used a call adapted in the language of the market: 'Leeks and Peas'. The campaign was successful.

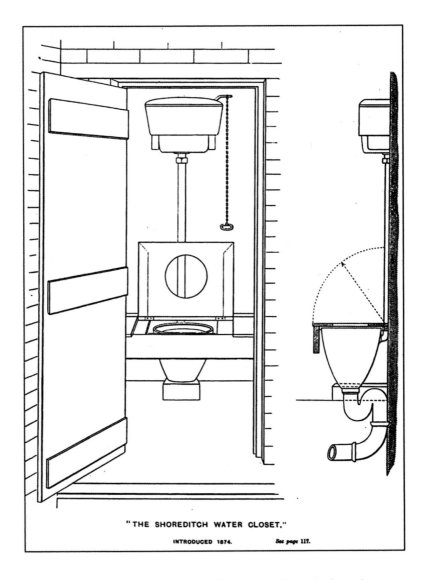

"THE SHOREDITCH WATER CLOSET."

INTRODUCED 1874.   *See page 117.*

Hardship created generations of fighters in Shoreditch, right up to the present day. Shoreditch has produced at least two Members of Parliament: George Jeger was Mayor of Shoreditch in 1937 and went on to become an MP. Bryan Magee, MP, wrote of his Hoxton childhood in 'Clouds of Glory'.

The Tenants and Residents Associations (TRAs) have championed local people over the years. In Fellows Court, the TRA Room is named after Dolly Pearson, who ran the hall for many years for local residents,

above Carole Young (on the left) with Winnie Ames and Marie McCourt in 2001.

unpaid, following in the tradition of Reg and Joyce Fry. Jackie Carter now does the honours and this is repeated again and again on estates across Shoreditch. Unfortunately there is no space here to pay tribute by name to all those working tirelessly and voluntarily for a better community and a better Shoreditch. But two close friends and allies merit particular mention: Carole Young and Peggy Edwards. Their fight was for a better deal after Shoreditch Borough was merged into the London Borough of Hackney in 1965. They both served one term as local councillors. Carole Young, 1942-2006, lived on Arden then Cranston Estate. She would often be forced to ask "Have I got mug stamped on my forehead" and didn't hold back in telling officials their pet ideas were "bollocks" when faced with bureaucracy and laxitude. Carole was the Shoreditch Festival organiser from 1983. Carole was instrumental in the formation of Shoreditch Trust in 2000 and its chair for several years. A bench in Shoreditch Park is dedicated to 'Carole Young – Woman of Hoxton and Champion of Shoreditch Park'.

The following is typical of the daily contribution made to improve living conditions. On the Arden Estate in the mid 1980s, where Peggy Edwards lived, a collapsed water pipe led to a plague of rats. The Council officer arrived and met Peggy at the offending hole. Standing over it, on cue, a rat popped out. The man from the Council said, with all seriousness "the problem is, is that a Hackney rat or a GLC rat". Quick as a flash, Peggy responded: "I don't know. Why don't you ask for his bleedin' rent book?"

Peggy gave this account of her new flat on Arden: "If this is what luxury is, well, it is unbelievable. The cupboards are falling down, the ceiling's collapsing, doors are falling off, and leaks cannot be found as pipes are hidden, you get these in a Kenny Everett Show or That's Life or Monty Python. I have even got a porthole in the toilet so I can converse with my next door neighbour when she is in her kitchen."

● Deputy Mayor Peggy Edwards (second from left) with friends from the Regal Way Pensioners' Club.

above Peggy Edwards, second from left, in the Hackney Gazette in the 1980s.

Lack of care and dereliction extended way beyond housing, and onto the streets. A notable recent example was the Pitfield Street roundabout, outside St John's Church. About five years ago, it was a neglected mess of weeds and rubble. Sick of the impression this gave of the area, a sign appeared overnight on the eyesore. It was beautifully made and fittingly announced 'Hackney's Entry in the Britain in Bloom Competition'. Marie McCourt and Maureen Walker were not available for comment!

Bombs, pets and dirty crockery

"You always had war looking at you." Mark Brooks said, and how true that was for the last century. The docks may have been hammered by bombing, but St Leonard's Hospital saw the first air-raid casualties of WWII on September 9th 1940 and was itself bombed in 1941. Naturally, everyone who was alive at that time recalled the impact of war. Nestling next to the City of London, it was no surprise that Shoreditch had its share of incidents.

On Hoxton Street itself, the biggest loss perhaps was the Britannia Theatre and Pollock's Toy Shop nearby. In Haggerston, the Imperial Gas Works was hit and St Mary's Church destroyed. But there were small and larger bomb sites everywhere – each one representing a tragedy. The population in Shoreditch more than halved between 1931 and 1951. Joyce Howes reflects on the number of people she knew before the war: "half of them never came back."

In Wenlock, one of the worst incidents became known as the 'Terror of Wenlock Brewery'. Joyce Howes tells of this tragedy where she lost both her uncle and cousin, called Alf and Alfie. Alfie had a disability and his father bravely stayed in the carnage to help his son, but both died of their injuries a few days later. The following is based on an account of that night on September 19th 1940 by

left The site of the Britannia Theatre in Hoxton Street after bomb damage.

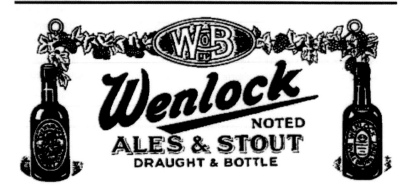

above Wenlock Brewery beer sign.

Stephen Sadler. The large basement of Wenlock Brewery was made a public air raid shelter early in the war. At the height of the Blitz, several hundred people went down there. They tried to keep their spirits up, although they could hear bombs screeching down on their homes and around the brewery. A direct hit on the school next door sent debris flying over the brewery, blocking all the exits and trapping those inside. The brewery was also hit and the large refrigeration plant started to leak ammonia. A group in one part of the building, working together using brute force, managed to break through the street skylight, but the largest group was trapped and choking on the ammonia gas and dust. There was blind panic as people fought to find relatives and a way out of the hell hole. At last, the rescuers broke through and a door was opened, but the rush towards it caused many to be trampled, adding to those already fatally affected by the gas. The deaths are recorded on a memorial in Holy Trinity Church.

Enormous tanks of water were built on street corners to put out fires caused by bombing. St Mary's Hostel in Hoxton Street provided the base for fire wardens and the police to deal with fire raids. Franny Sydes recalled the police coming down Hoxton Street from Old Street Police Station "with sandwich boards saying 'All Clear' or 'Take Cover' during air raids. In Wilkes Place, elderly chaps stood with a square lamp which had a red slide for 'Enemy Alert' or green slide for 'All Clear'."

Betty Kemp was nine when the family was bombed out of Alma Street (now Cherbury Street). "I think you'll find it was one of the first land mines. We were in the house as war hadn't properly started. The war had been phoney up until then. I ended up going into St Leonard's Hospital as I had St Vitus Dance. Everyone else in the family was alright." St Vitus Dance is usually caused by an infection – maybe this was really trauma in such a young child. Betty, though, grew and thrived. She was evacuated. Her poor mother was bombed out again, but she too survived.

Gwen Plume recalls sheltering from the bombs underneath the Gas Light and Coke Company's premises nearby. Luckily, Gwen was not there in 1944 when a doodlebug hit the works, destroying both it and a good part of the surrounding area.

Joyce Howes was thirteen when the war started. The family prepared her for evacuation, and her name was sewn into all her clothes. But she refused to go, so spent the war in London. She'd help the men fill sandbags and used Old Street Station as a bomb shelter, together with many others. The bedding would be rolled out when the trains stopped running about 11.00pm, but there wouldn't be much sleep as Joyce explains: "We had some laughs down there. If it wasn't such a bad thing, we had a great time. Younger children didn't realise so much what was happening. To them it was like a little party." Tea in flasks and soft drinks would get passed round, people would tell stories, play cards and sing. She'd get up every morning for school in the usual way – the authorities were very strict about going to school and sent a letter home to say she had to go back to school when she stopped going. One day, Joyce was in bed with flu in the family's flat in Great Eastern Street. She was too ill to get to the station when the aircraft warning went. An incendiary bomb hit the factory next door, just the other side of the wall from her bed, and burnt it down. If it had been a normal bomb, she would be dead. They still had to carry her out as she was too ill to get out by herself.

Also in the thick of it was Peggy Crowe, who lived with her family on Redvers Street, part of the labyrinth of streets and alleyways behind the Macbeth Pub. She and her family used to shelter beneath the Chippendale Furniture factory, one of the many in the area. As overcrowded as the houses were, being packed in the shelters brought both comfort and discomfort. It re-enforced the

shared community, but not without problems. "An old lady who used the shelter had an alarm that went off at six every morning; it woke the whole shelter up." Peggy's father wasn't best pleased they stayed in Shoreditch anyway, as he thought it unsafe. He was on the anti-aircraft guns on the East Anglian Coast. Peggy's mother refused to consider evacuation, but she did agree to go to another shelter. "Mum wouldn't let the youngsters be evacuated, she'd say 'If we are going to see it through, we are going to see it through together. If I go, who will want my kids?'"

Peggy continued "The Fishnets, the boot menders, were Jewish and lived at the bottom of Falkirk Street. I was friendly with one of the daughters because she used to sleep next to me in the shelter. One night they dropped a bomb by the entrance in Drysdale Street. Nan had gone down with the kids just after six when the sirens went. Me and my mum went later with jugs of cocoa. Cissie Fishnet ran outside and fell in a crater and an ambulance ran over her and killed her."

Peggy's bombing saga was far from over. Her account of what happened next is worth recounting in full. It shows the disruption to lives wreaked by the war. It also shows how much organisation and support was provided by the authorities.

"In Redvers Street, we had back yards with some grass. On Bank Holiday, August 1944, it was at the beginning of August then, a doodle bug fell in the bottom of my garden and we were bombed out. Me and Harry (her then fiancé) were off bicycling, we were going camping and the family were coming to join us. Anyhow, they never turned up. My sister came though and told us what had happened. Mum said she saw a ball of flame in the sky. It was a direct hit on Jaycole, who made berets and was at the back of the Labour Exchange nearby. My mum tried to dive under the table to save herself. The ambulances came round followed by the RSPCA vans, because everyone had animals."

"My sister Rosie and another were at the Odeon Picture House on Hackney Road. On the screen comes up, so and so street got hit. The kid's done no more than run back for her dolls. My younger brother ran home too. The Warden tried to stop them, but neighbours said they lived there. Mum had a friend staying with us; her family had been evacuated to Oxford. The ambulance took her all the way to Oxford. We were camping at Rickmansworth; the men went back to London and brought the family to the camp."

"After we went back to London we went to get our stuff back. The tablecloth was full of broken crockery and dirty from the dinner they'd been eating when the bomb dropped. The authorities had just tied it up and put it in storage. Just like that."

"I worked in Hatton Garden at that time and we were engaged, so I stayed in London. But this time the children and my mum went to Wales. My mum's sister was a housekeeper for someone in Carmarthen. There was a cottage going in the grounds she could use. Women didn't go into pubs, but my mum did. There were no nearby shops so they had to go into Carmarthen which was over ten miles away. Food vans used to come to the square outside the pub and you'd go with your ration books for provisions. She didn't last long, she came back to Hoxton."

"We'd got a house for them to come back to. We'd just put the curtains up when a flying bomb came down and they were bombed out again so they went to live with Harry (Peggy's husband) in Howe (now Hale) Street in a flat. He made the beds like a shelter in the basement. Put tree trunks in to hold the roof up and nails in the tree trunks to hang our clothes on. We lasted out the rest of the war like that. Trees are great things. St Margaret's Church came down, three foot square solid cubes, but the trees that surrounded it are still standing."

This experience was echoed by many an adult evacuee: women from this part of London were freer to run their own lives than those in rural areas. Young evacuees had mixed experiences. Edie and Pat Murphy were both evacuated as teenagers. Pat found it harder as they split him and his brothers up in different houses. Edie went to Berkshire, near an American camp with Italian prisoners of war. She remembers the Italian prisoners as kind to the kids, giving then 'cookies'. Irene Cakebread had a raw deal as an evacuee in Nottingham; Mavis, the woman who took her in, took the money her mother sent to her. Sometimes, she had to sleep under the stairs in a cupboard full of glass cases full of stuffed animals. Returning to Shoreditch after the war, Hoxton market had changed little, despite the bombing. It still had most of the same shopkeepers and stallholders.

above Wasteland along Queensbridge Road created by bombing. Photo taken in the mid 80s prior to the development of the Haggerston Park extension.

Peggy's work was in Hatton Garden, centre of the jewellery industry. She had wanted to do war work so she was sent to the Fine Wire Department located in one of the major jewellery workshops. "One of the jobs I had was like cutting tin foil, but it was thick. It was about half inch wide and everything was precision measured. I never found out what it was for until later. Bagfuls were dropped from planes to confuse radar when we were bombing Europe."

Coming down Pearson Street one day with her family, Tom Carlow's mum heard a doodlebug dropping and then the scary sound of its engine stopping, which meant it was close. There was a men's urinal nearby, so she gathered the children up and charged inside for shelter. As she'd never been in one before, she didn't know it had no roof and therefore provided little protection. Looking up, she was shocked to see the bomb pass over their heads.

Not everyone was so lucky. Joyce Howes started work at the age of fourteen. During the war, she worked in a printers, gumming envelopes. She had to sign the Official Secrets Act as some of the letters were to those who had a relative killed in action. Her husband, Philip, fought at Monte Casino in Italy alongside a man called Freddie Philip Howse. One day, Joyce received one of the envelopes she had been gumming to say her husband had been killed. Luckily for her but tragically for Freddie's family, she'd already had a letter from him to say he was injured, but that Freddie had been killed.

Irene Cakebread lived with her parents at her grandmother's house in Grange Street during the war. One night, she went out with her mother to get some beer for her father, who was a fireman. They stopped off to get some chips. On the way home, her mother looked up, saw a doodlebug, and rammed her into a doorway. The bomb fell just behind their house, wrecking it. There was broken glass everywhere. Irene says: "All I could think to say was – I got glass in my chips." The family had to live in bomb shelters until the house was fixed up enough to live in.

Rationing continued throughout the war and into the early 1950s. One day, Tom Carlow was in his pram in Hoxton Street, when a cry of "bananas" went out. All the women charged off, including his mother, to get some. On arriving home with the treasured booty, she realised she'd left her other treasure behind. He was still in his pram in the market "happy as Larry". Mary Walker worked at Gunners the butchers. She remembers rationing and people asking if they could "have it off next week's" book, hoping to get a bit extra. People would also try and rub out the cross on the ration book if it was done in pencil.

Rationing led to hoarding, often of peculiar things. Tom remembers his mother had a wardrobe full of icing sugar – but "she'd never iced a cake in her life". When they moved house in 1954, the sugar was still there.

People from Shoreditch certainly did their bit in the war, both on the front line and at home. But there is another side: if the authorities were organised, so was the black market. Mary Walker remembers a man used to come door to door selling black market tea in white paper bags. Her mum stocked up, saying "Well, at least we'll be alright for tea now". Hoxton Street market was no stranger to this kind of trade; it was the way you survived. Certain local families had their reputations as being 'suppliers' of goods for those with a bit of spare cash or gold. Things 'falling off' the back of boats, lorries, or out of factories was a way of life. It was all seen just as what you did. No questions asked, and be grateful someone was doing you a favour.

I'd rather graft than do nothing

In the 19th and most of the 20th Centuries, Shoreditch was an industrial centre: printing, box-making, clothes, footwear and haberdashery manufacture, leather chandlery and glass making were major trades, and still have a presence today. But the biggest employer by far was the furniture trade.

The Regent's Canal was a living organ for transporting goods to and from the area, into the middle of the last century. And this brought timber, lots of timber, which made Shoreditch the leading furniture making area in London up to about 30 years ago. The City Sawmills in New North Road and the Eagle Saw Mills in Wenlock Basin were the largest of several saw mills and timber yards. With furniture-making came a range of associated specialist skills and suppliers of materials, such as fabrics, iron and brass work, springs, locks and glass for doors.

Every type and quality of furniture was produced in Shoreditch. In recognition of Shoreditch as the centre for furniture production, the London County Council created the Technical Institute in Pitfield Street in 1893, with courses in every branch of furniture and upholstery manufacture and design. It was the first of its kind in London.

left *Lucas Furniture Co. Ltd in Dunloe Street, 1959.*

above Tyzack Tool Shop advert from The Woodworker, 1956.

Henry Tyzack, a sawmaker from Sheffield, set up shop in Shoreditch in 1839. The Tyzack family had shops locally in Old Street, New North Road and Kingsland Road (which remains) selling a huge variety of tools used in woodworking and other trades. Their main competitors were Parry's.

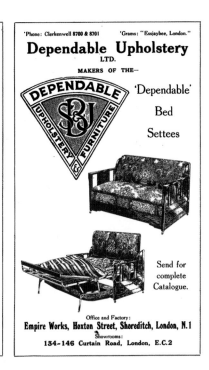
above Adverts from the 1930 Shoreditch Guide.

next 1930 Shoreditch Guide advert for Janeshore Motors.

The presence of these trades and products gave rise to a whole generation of men who were fitters. People like John Sawyer, who travelled the country as a fitter and joiner. His father represented the prior generation of workers, having a stall on the slim sliver of pavement known as 'The Waste' on Kingsland Road. John took his father's boxes of screws to sell. Nobody went near them, so John mixed them up in buckets and sold them at five shillings (25p) a handful. The cost worked out about the same but the art was in the psychology of the sale.

Notable large local companies include Goddard and Gibbs, a spectacular stained glass factory in Kingsland Road. The firm moved there in 1946 and made stained glass windows for all over the world, winning the Queen's Award for Industry. It ran a successful apprentice scheme up to its move to Stratford in the 1990s. Scandalously, the listed building was bulldozed by the developer and Shoreditch lost one of its finest industrial buildings.

Foxes specialised in safe installation and removal. Based in Hoxton Square for about a century, it employed generations of local people until moving in order to expand at the beginning of this century.

Less well known is that Shoreditch became a centre for motor transport before mass production, which required huge factories, took over. This followed the local tradition of making horse transport and cartage – cart making. There were also rubber works locally, such as the Universal Rubber Company at 34-36 Kingsland Road, to make tyres. Bespoke cars and vans were made in the days before mass production, and Shoreditch could turn its hand to anything.

People from Shoreditch have formed their own businesses, sometimes in retail, sometimes in local warehouses or in manufacturing. Pat Murphy worked for his Uncle Ted for a time. Ted was a gifted artist. He set up his own business making intricate Christmas decorations in a factory in Kingsland Road.

Joyce Howes' parents ran the newspaper stall outside the London Apprentice in Old Street. Her mother's family came from Norfolk and had a tradition of working in the royal households of Sandringham and Buckingham Palace. But Joyce's gran put a stop to that saying she was not letting her daughter "work as a skivvy for nothing". Joyce's father came to Shoreditch from Scotland in his teens to join his brother. On arriving, he got his first ever footwear, a pair of brown boots. For the rest of his life, he only wore brown boots "so shiny you could see your face in them". He also wore brown suits. This earned him the nickname of 'Brownie' in Hoxton Street Market, which he'd walk through selling papers.

People from Shoreditch have had successful careers in all the fields. In early days, Edmund Halley, the Astronomer Royal who identified and thus named Halley's Comet, came from Haggerston. Thomas Fairchild, 'the Father of the Flower Garden', was the original city gardener. A nurseryman and scientific botanist, he ran the equivalent of a modern nursery and garden centre in Ivy Lane, Hoxton, in the late 1600s and early 1700s. He was the first person to create a hybrid plant known as Fairchild's Mule. Although few so illustrious, some of Shoreditch's own have gone into one of the fields of science. Betty's brother, Jim, went to night school and qualified as a Chartered Mechanical Engineer. He travelled the world with his profession, working for a large firm in the City.

But for many, work was often hard to find, and hard when found. Mark Brooks wrote this poem, reflecting many a Shoreditch working life.

Birds sing at the close of a day
As the sun settles and the moon finds its own way
As one sits thinking of the past day
Over the boredom and drudgeries of living this way
Working, working, living day to day
No prospects of wealth or fame to come my way
But in my head, my dreams no one can take away
For at the close of each day
I shut my eyes and fly away

People would turn their hand to anything, and many were constantly in and out of employment. There was little job security. This was a pattern set from the earliest times: in the furniture trade, a carpenter would get enough money for timber for one chair, then hawk it round the warehouses to sell it to make a little bit and buy more wood for the next chair. If he didn't sell it, the family didn't eat. Later, different components, such as the legs or seat, of a chair would be made by one carpenter in his house and then taken to the factory to put together. It could be said that ducking and diving was, and is, a major Shoreditch occupation. If local networks didn't come up with anything, people would walk round the streets looking for 'help wanted' signs.

Up to the 1960s, even skilled workers would have work for maybe two or three days a week, then have to sign on for the others. The furniture and rag trades especially worked this way. Joyce Howes' husband was a skilled presser, but he was still 'in and out of work like a yo-yo', even though the same tailor would have him back again and again when there was a job on. They had just about enough money to pay the rent and eat, but often had to rely on the family to help out.

Youngsters would earn the odd penny or shilling doing odd jobs in the markets, helping to clear up factories or workshops, picking stray threads off clothes or helping to deliver things. Those with parents doing piece work (payment by the piece) at home would routinely help out – stuffing envelopes, sewing, making things like crackers

right Hows Wood Factory, 1955.

above Steve Noe (bottom right), Alan Shea (top right) and Ricky Noe (next to Alan) with friends, 1980s. Steve and Ricky ran Pinewood Videos in Hoxton Street.

or rosettes. Betty Kemp's mother represents workers of bygone times. She was a home worker making satin lined chocolate boxes, which were a real work of art. Betty recalls her mum melting chunks of glue in a black pot on the range in their kitchen, before using small brushes to glue and then construct the boxes which graced the very best confectioners. One wonders in these health and safety obsessed times what would be made of the bubbling glue pot next to the Sunday roast!

Tom Carlow's family's employment was pretty typical. His father was a French polisher, and then worked at Spitalfields meat market. His mother did the same as Betty's, trimming boxes for a small, local firm. Sometimes, she went into the workshop, other times she'd do the work at home, with the family helping out. If Tom was home from school for any reason, she might take him into work with her and he'd help out gluing and trimming. The work suited a woman with a young family, as she could vary the hours. Tom's brother worked as an engineer and his sister Flossie put gold blocking on autograph books and photo albums.

Irene Cakebread's father was a French polisher, while she went to work for a local printer. When her firm moved to Suffolk, she and her family were offered a house there. Her father was keen to go, but her mother refused as she said "there's too much green".

Warehouses and factories along the canal provided numerous jobs for local people, as well as goods, both officially and unofficially. A printer on the north side of the canal by Whitmore Bridge used to print the Marvel comic. Local boys would go down each week to be given a free copy.

above Alan Shea with young people from the Colville Estate youth club he runs. From right: Marvella, Alan, Collie, Sydney, Madiana, Te, Jenebo, Anna, Mary. They made a giant fag cut by the Speaker at the opening of an NHS community event, 2007.

Alan Shea ran both fruit and vegetable stalls and a shop selling 'pick and mix' in Hoxton Street in the 1980s. He'd get up at 1am to go to buy stock, make up orders, then make deliveries to caterers as well as individual homes, then set up the stall and serve all day, then do the books and fall into bed at 9pm. And this was seven days a week. He even went to farms in Essex to buy direct from the farmers. Asked how he coped working all the hours, he says "I'd rather graft than do nothing".

Of course, some jobs were not always legal. Crime featured locally, as everywhere. There are those born in Shoreditch whose careers have taken them to the wrong side of the law. People talked about a particular group of women in the 1950s who would meet up to wait for their children at the school gates. This group of women were always exquisitely dressed, unlike the rest of the mothers waiting for their broods. This was a cause for much discussion among the other mothers. It transpired that one of these women worked for Shirley Pitts, a local girl who hit the headlines as the most successful shoplifter, possibly of all time. The book of her life, 'Gone Shopping', tells all. Shirley and her 'girls' focused their attention on big West End Stores like Harrods but made 'shopping' expeditions as far afield as Paris, Geneva and Berlin.

Born in 1934, Shirley had become the adult of the family aged seven when her dad was sent to jail. To survive, she started off by thieving bread from doorsteps and coal from coal-carts. She died in 1992, and the most famous faces of the criminal underworld were present at her funeral. Even the Kray twins, who started off in Crondal Street, sent their condolences. Fourteen 'Rollers' accompanied the coffin to the graveside and a huge floral tribute in the shape of a Harrods bag carried the epitaph 'Gone Shopping'. She was buried in an expensive dress, specially stolen for the occasion.

Shirley wasn't the first of her ilk. Writing of her memories of 1910, the late Grace Blacketer recalled a felon who stood out from the rest, one Dinkie, a bookmaker's widow. Dinkie worked 'the Nile', the small market on Nile Street. She was far from dinkie however, being a large corseted lump. Primarily she was a moneylender, with a retinue of thugs to make sure the loan repayments were kept up to date. Anyone seen about with a broken limb was suspected of being 'a dinkie'. Dinkie could fix almost anything, at a price, including people on the run. She could hide you, organise abortions for unwanted pregnancies, and sort out any problems you had, if you could afford her. When she died in the late 19th century she was reputedly worth half a million pounds.

Fictional crime, too, was a nice little earner for some locals. Perhaps, not having to look far for role models, people like George

above Stocks in Shoreditch Churchyard for criminals from an earlier time.

Sewell (1924-2007) brought a villainous presence to television and cinema screens for many years. Up to the age of thirty five, George had an eclectic range of jobs, including working as an assistant to a French roller-skating team. But a chance meeting with actor Dudley Sutton in a pub set him on the path to Joan Littlewood's Theatre Workshop, and thence on to celluloid fame in films like 'Get Carter' and TV series such as 'Z Cars'. Given that he grew up with England's then premier film studios on his doorstep, it's in keeping that his career veered in that direction.

Gainsborough Studios, by the canal on Poole Road, started off as a power station for the Metropolitan Electric Railway, before becoming a centre of film-making from 1921. Silent movies were made there, and then talkies. One film, 'The Camels are Coming' had desert scenes filmed on the roof which was covered with sand carried manually up and then back down again. The Gainsborough Studio's most famous artist was Alfred Hitchcock, who started his career there in the props department. It subsequently became a warehouse – notably Kelaty's, piled high with oriental carpets, in the 1970s and 1980s. It has now been largely demolished and re-built as flats. The new development has a giant sculpture of Hitchcock's head as its centrepiece.

above The Gainsborough's "Master of Suspense" sculpture.
right Marie Lloyd.

With the Gainsborough Studios just around the corner, it seemed natural when someone mentioned that Hitchcock's 1935 film 'The 39 Steps' had been partly filmed in Hoxton Hall. And Haggerston Park's north gate features in the 1940s film 'Odd Man Out' with James Mason. Edie Murphy's mother and father were Pearly King and Queen. They appear as themselves singing 'Any Old Iron' in the film 'London Town' with Kay Kendal. Local hardman, Lenny McLean, played Barry the Baptist in 'Lock, Stock and Two Smoking Barrels'. There is now even a film named 'Shoreditch', made a couple of years back, starring Joely Richardson and Shane Ritchie.

Shoreditch continues to have significant links with the film industry, from model making to animation. Entertainers have left their mark down the centuries. Shakespeare and his cronies may have been some of the first, but they were certainly not the last to visit the area. Other, more home grown, are familiar faces.

Marie Lloyd was a favourite of the Music Halls and an early Shoreditch superstar. One of nine children, she was born Matilda Wood in 1870 in Plumber Street, Hoxton. She was famous for risqué songs, often accompanied by a saucy wink, which the public loved but which was not approved of in high places. She also stood up for the rights of lesser known performers. Many of her songs are still known today, such as 'My Old Man' and 'A Little Bit of What You Fancy (does you good)'. Less well known songs of the era include one with the chorus: "A nice piece of fish, served on a dish, are soles, are soles, are soles". Another, with the opening line "Husbands are dustbins" has the memorable line "With them and their habits, I'd rather keep rabbits".

Matt Monroe, 1930-1985, was born Terry Parsons in Shoreditch. He worked as a bus driver, among other jobs, in the 1950s. However, by 1961, he had been named Top International Act by Billboard magazine. He went on to record such famous songs as 'Softly As I Leave You', and the film theme songs for 'From Russia with Love' and 'Born Free'.

Barbara Windsor was born in Shoreditch in 1937, the daughter of a costermonger and a seamstress. Like George Sewell, Barbara is another product of Joan Littlewood's Theatre Workshop. Her intelligence and talent saw her make her stage debut at thirteen and her first film role in the 'The Belles of St Trinian's' in 1954. Now a national treasure, Babs has seldom been off our screens.

Birds of a Feather stars, Pauline Quirk & Linda Robson, used to work as Saturday girls in a Hoxton Street dry cleaners.

The debate about whether Shoreditch is in the East End or North London continues, but it certainly has links with EastEnders. Barbara Windsor is now a firm favourite in the series as Peggy Mitchell. Shoreditch actor, Peter Dean, played the soap's first fruit and veg stallholder, Pete Beale. Julie Harris, now Patsy Palmer who plays Bianca, comes from Bethnal Green, but spent many a Thursday night at the White Horse pub Karaoke sessions in the 1980s, before fame came along.

And local people were employed in other jobs in the film industry. Alan Shea's father worked in film units back in the 1970s and 80s as a stuntman, driver, extra and all sorts. Alan was one of the kids seen in the first edition of Minder 'Gunfight at the OK Launderette'. While the producer got the other kids to skip, Alan can be seen resolutely in a tough guy pose.

Some locals came even nearer to the film experience when films were made about them. Melek came to the UK when she was eight years old. She was pivotal in the making of a documentary about the lives of people like herself who came from Cyprus by boat over half a century ago. She is reflective of the communities within communities which exemplify the older immigrant experience. She is settled, and very much part of the local scene, yet retaining her cultural heritage and respecting her roots.

right Melek Kazim, 2009.

A little of what you fancy

Shoreditch loves to let its hair down. In the Elizabethan age, the area around Hoxton Street had a number of tea or pleasure gardens attracting visitors from the City into what was then the countryside. The Pimlico Gardens stood near Fanshaw Street and was spoken about by Ben Johnson as the resort of the poets and players of the period. The Grecian, which became the Eagle Tavern, lasted the longest, with Charles Dickens singing its praises. As well as strolls and picnics, the gardens provided entertainment with drama, concerts, fireworks, clowns, acrobats and puppet shows such as Punch and Judy. There were sports ranging from bowls and skittles to riding and wrestling.

Ever since James Burbage built the first London playhouse in Curtain Road in 1576, Shoreditch has enjoyed theatres: at the turn of the 19th century, there was the Standard in Shoreditch High Street, later the Cirque Olympian; the Varieties in Pitfield Street built in 1870, Hoxton Hall and the Britannia, among others, including the dubious penny gaffs.

left *Britannia Music Hall in Hoxton Street, around 1920.*

Monday, Dec. 30th, 1912.

Ladies are respectfully requested to remove their Hats so as to afford greater comfort to the persons seated behind.

1 **OVERTURE**

2 **GWENNIE HASTO**
In Quaint Songs and Fancy Dances

3 **FRANK ARMSTRONG**
In his Vocal and Protean Act.

4 **Mr. JAMES WILLARD & Co.**
In Famous Sketch
"THE ACE OF HEARTS"
Or, "Thou Shalt not Covet Thy Neighbour's Wife."
By JAMES WILLARD.
John Fairburn, a Journalist ... ... Mr. FRED WILSON
'Lola Vane,' an Actress, his Wife ... Miss DOLLY BISHOP
Dick Royston, their Friend ... Mr. JAMES WILLARD
SCENE Fairburn's Flat in London

5 **WALTER EMERSON**
The Original 6 Feet of Comicality

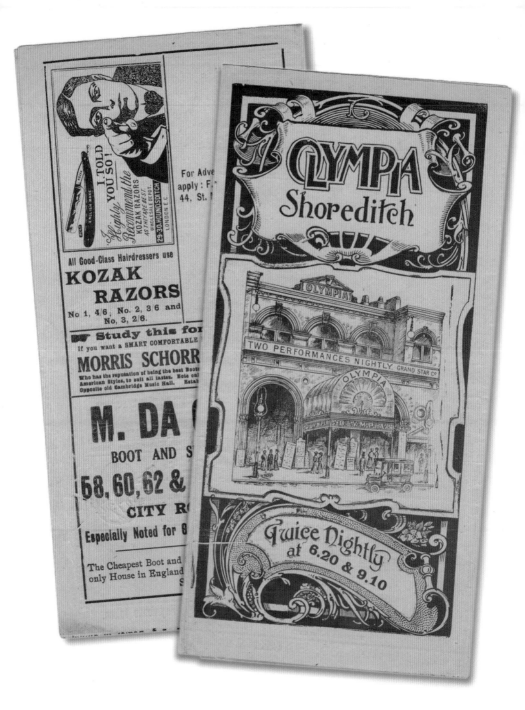

previous & above Olympia Music Hall on Shoreditch High Street programme, 1912.

left from the Britannia pantomime programme for the Magic Dragon of the Demon Dell.

The biggest, and arguably most popular, music hall in North East London was the Britannia (The Brit). This was on Hoxton Street between Fanshaw Street and Myrtle Walk. Opened in 1841, it had 4000 seats and was highly decorated with gold leaf. Pantomime, melodrama, comedy, opera, variety shows and Shakespeare were enjoyed by local residents and the likes of Charles Dickens. Dickens wrote at length in praise of every aspect of the theatre from cleanliness to its sandwiches, and compared it to La Scala in Milan "lighted by a firmament of sparkling chandeliers". The owner, after her husband died, was authoress and actress, Sara Lane, dubbed 'the Queen of Hoxton'. When she died in 1899, the funeral procession went along Hoxton Street. The crowds were so thick you couldn't get through and shops closed for the day in tribute.

The first film show was given at the Britannia in 1899 and it became mainly a cinema between the two World Wars. Sadly destroyed by enemy action in 1940, the site is commemorated by a blue plaque today.

Luckier is Hoxton Hall, one of the few intact music halls still standing. In its heyday, run by May Scott in the 1970s, it inspired many local youngsters to get involved in the arts. Rumour has it that the artists Gilbert and George started off in Hoxton Hall. Bob and Mick Walker also put their Hoxton Hall training to good use: they fund-raised for Shoreditch Festival by going round the pubs singing 'Don't Cry for me, Argentina' – being paid to shut up!

Henry Browne recounted how, at the age of nine, he won singing competitions at the Britannia and Hoxton Cinema in Pitfield Street. Whether it was 'Marie Eleanor' or 'I, I, I, I, I, I Love You Very Much', he never failed to win, especially when his mates in the audience had 3d each to clap. Or it might have been the bowl of fruit on his head which clinched it.

above Bob and Mick Walker, with 'Sam', in Phillipp Street, 1967.

As Pat Murphy says, "there were cinemas everywhere". Tom Carlow says "you could see a different film every day of the week in Shoreditch." There was the Standard in Goldsmiths Row, the Hoxton in Pitfield Street, the Odeon in Hackney Road and a whole row of them in Kingsland Road. And there were also the scams to try and get in free. Edie Murphy remembers kids sitting on each other's shoulders with a big overcoat over the top to get two in on one ticket. Other times, one would pay and then let the others in through the back entrance. The group at Mr Samwidges enjoyed Saturday morning cinema, especially the cowboy films. Parents were relieved to be child-free for a break and children lapped up the cartoons and films for little money. Others remember brothers and sisters being named after screen idols – maybe conceived while the children were at the cinema themselves.

Holidays and outings used to be few and far between so people made the most of them. Even holidays, for some, involved work: hop picking in Kent was a means of getting away for people with no money to spare. It worked well if the weather was good, but not if it rained. Pat Murphy remembers being huddled together in a Nissen hut with the deafening sound of rain on the tin roof.

above A day trip to Hastings in the 1920s with
Elsie Crowe, Peggy Crowe's sister, second from the left.

Schools, Sunday schools and the Missions organised the outings for many locals. The Costers Hall Christian Mission, next to Wilmer Gardens, was one such. It laid on day trips to places like Littlehampton, Southend and Clacton. For individual children and families, there was Epping Forest, Hampstead Heath, as well as the coast.

above Women from the Hunt family, said to be the biggest family in Hoxton, on a beano to Margate in the 1930s.

By the 1950s, with almost full employment and the beginnings of the package holiday industry, people had money to venture further. Betty Kemp was nineteen when she first went abroad in 1950 with her pal Doris. They went to Ostend but, over the years, their travels took them far and wide. Tossa del Mar was a working fishing village when they visited it. Betty first went to Florida aged 60, where she fell in love with Disney World. Likewise, later, when visiting Las Vegas. She's still an avid traveller all these years later. Kay Stone, one of the St Mary's Estate ladies, and her entrepreneur husband Jack went one further, buying a hotel in Belgium.

Because of his lineage, Mark Brooks had deeper connections abroad: "When I was 18, my father and I walked from Italy into Switzerland. There were tiny villages, no roads just tracks. Everyone we met turned their face to the wall as we walked past, in case you were a smuggler, see. They could say they never saw you. This was in 1968 and mountain men lived in peat igloos. They had blond or ginger hair. They talked to us asking where were our guns? It was October and apparently the wolves were coming down from the mountain and they were hungry. You've never seen two men come down a mountain so fast in your life."

above Pat Shea with a friend on the holiday to
Los Angeles she won at the Hackney Road Bingo Hall.

PASTIMES

Pastimes are as varied as people in the area. Tom Carlow's house in Hows Street had a cellar which was re-enforced with concrete during the war as an air raid shelter. After the war, it was declared unsafe, but Tom's father found many uses for it. He mended shoes, did carpentry and incubated hens' eggs. He'd sell the newly hatched chickens to neighbours and also took them to Club Row. He kept chickens in the back yard and "dad would breed and kill them, the children would pluck them and my mother would clean and cook them. Then we'd all have chicken for dinner."

Jo Dorking's family in Essex Street also had animals around. "Dad would often pick up animals such as ducks and ferrets. When my dad was small, he went to Brick Lane and brought three chicks for sixpence – a tanner. He took them home and hid them in his wardrobe. It wasn't long before his mother found them and got them out. They was following her all round the flat as they thought she was their mother. When my dad arrived home from school, he was told to get rid of them. Upset, he headed to his Nan's house, Ginnie's, who lived above Levers, a clothes shop on the corner of Purcell Street. His Nan already had a bird aviary. His Nan said: "Sure boy you can keep them here." The chicks grew huge and the black chick was a massive cockerel that used to jump off the balcony and run up Hoxton Market. People would often be seen carrying Ginnie's black cockerel back home to her."

above Nelie Neale's backyard full of animals in Shaftsbury Street, 1946.

It's lucky that John Sawyer was a fitter and joiner as he has been able to build the cabinets and boxes in which he keeps his acquisitions. His hobby is collecting, anything. Not only that, he can also fix anything. At 80, he still maintains the block of flats in which he lives. You can hardly move in his flat for objects. He has a half century old New World gas cooker which is pristine and in use every day.

Many of his prized possessions come from his other hobby, metal detecting. He has coins from just about every period of British history, and a few oddities. One day, whilst prospecting in the sandy bottom of a stream, he heard loud beeps. Reaching down he picked up a muddy, grimy object. Much to his surprise, it was an 18th century set of false teeth, mounted on an 18 carat gold plate and stuck together with vulcanite. Today it gleams as new. John reckons it was a lady's and postulates that she may have taken a tumble from a horse.

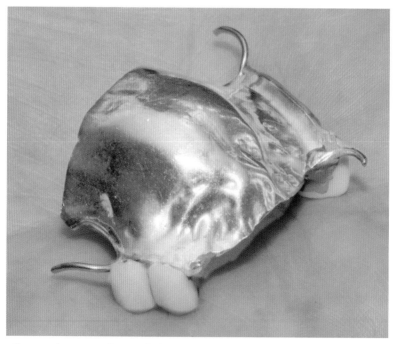

above John Sawyer's favourite find: a pair of gold false teeth.
right John Sawyer with a photo of his sweetheart, 2009.

Other tumbles come to mind with his next find. He opens a small tin, in which lies the now perished remnants of a condom. Apparently these boxes were standard issue to US troops going overseas in WWII. It seems that North East London woodlands are littered with them.

next Mary Walker (left) with her sister Joan and brothers John and Harry at a fair in the 1950s.

HAVING A FLUTTER

The sport of kings is a popular local pastime, a chance for a beano and, if you are lucky, a way to gain a few extra bob when and if your horse comes in. Charabancs, later coaches, would take people to the race meetings. It was a tradition for the families to gather round to see them off, and the men would throw any coppers out of their pockets to the waiting kids. If you were lucky, you might get some silver in there too. On a day to day basis, a local bet could keep hopes high and conversation going for hours.

Up until 1961, fantastic organisation and ingenuity went into the illegal betting trade, where big money could be made. Tom Carlow remembers going to place bets for his father in York Row. There'd be at least eight look-outs, plus the runners and the people taking the bet, making it a major operation. Tom was on his way to place a bet one day when he noticed "there was not a soul about. I saw the coppers coming, so I kept on walking."

George Square, where St Monica's School is now, was another base for illegal betting. Terry Briggs remembers that the police arrived one day, disguised as dustmen so they could get close. When the game was up, the ensuing chase went over the wall into Enfield Cloisters and off in all directions.

left A group of workers from the Nathan Meibvitz Company in Hoxton Square, embarking on a day out in a charabanc, 1920s. *above* Prince Monolulu.

It certainly sounds like getting a bet on was as much fun as the bet itself. When betting was made legal, the Hackney Gazette reported a 'Hoxton gent' saying "our street corner won't seem the same now without ol' 'arry leaning on the lamppost keeping an eye out for the coppers."

Ras Prince Monolulu (1881-1965) was almost an institution on the race scene from the 1920s. He was frequently seen in and around Shoreditch and the East End in his characteristic headgear and brightly coloured clothing. Essentially a tout, he took this rather shady profession to artistic heights. His real name was Peter Carl McKay. As a tipster promising a winner in return for payment, his best known call around the streets was "I gotta horse!" This was subsequently the title of his memoirs.

above Boxing class at Pitfield Street Baths in 1911.

SPORTING LIVES

Most sports have a long tradition in Shoreditch. The local football favourites are usually Tottenham or Arsenal (but rarely both!). Local man, John Pratt, was a Tottenham star of the 1970s. He ran a sweetshop in the shopping parade at the back of the Colville Estate – nicknamed Bonbons by locals – throughout the height of his career. Other local football heroes include Joe Wade (Arsenal), Bert Murray (Chelsea). Len Phillips (Portsmouth and England) and Chris Bart-Williams (Nottingham Forest).

The area has produced other champions. Brian Jacks won an Olympic gold medal in judo. Dave Starbrook from Wilmer Gardens was known locally as a gentle giant. He won an Olympic silver medal for judo. When he came home afterwards, the street and flats were all decorated to celebrate his success. Dave Sanderson was the World BMX Bunnyhop champion in the 1980s, jumping a massive forty two inches from the flat. Eddie Kidd trained in Shoreditch along the road where Britannia Leisure Centre is now. Another renowned local biker was Paul Hardcastle, who wrote the song '19' as well as the EastEnders tune. He and Eddie regularly raced each other around Shoreditch's waste grounds or along Queensbridge Road. John Shea got a special award when he won the Middlesex Darts Championship for three years on the run.

Fighting is a strong Shoreditch tradition. Boxing has been associated with the area since the late eighteenth century. Many boys first learnt to fight on the streets with each other. They might then join amateur training clubs at what were Boys Clubs, such as the Lion, St Monica's or Crown and Manor. These Boys Clubs now cater for both boys and girls. The sporting tradition stays strong for all their users.

The Lion Club was formed about 60 years ago. Sport is firmly on their agenda, but they also have a range of activities for young people. The Crown and Manor Club opened in its new premises in Wiltshire Row 1939, as an amalgamation of the Crown Club and the Hoxton Manor Club. Both Clubs were based in disused pubs before they joined together.

The Crown Club started off in 1926 in Ely Place, Hoxton. It was described in one of the first reports as 'a modest affair'. It had about 20 boys, all under 14, a tumble-down shed for headquarters and little else. Meetings were held one night a week and games were played on Saturdays. A club evening meant a carpentry class in a room about 10' square, and boxing and games like chess, draughts and ping pong in another room scarcely more than twice that size. Football matches were on a patch of gravel, with little equipment beside the ball. Hoxton Manor started off as the New North Road Club for Boys in 1903 and was the larger and better organised on the two, but charged a small fee for membership. In the following pages are some examples of the Club's regular football activities. The programmes illustrated are from the 1970s.

The Club is well known for its range of sporting achievements, but also has a tradition of drama, art and discussion groups, winning many awards.

following Crown & Manor football programmes from 1974 and 1971.

LUCKY 790

(PRIZE: Autographed ball by current Spurs & Arsenal players)

SHOREDITCH PARK   BRIDPORT PLACE
(OFF NEW NORTH ROAD)

CHARITY GAME

SUNDAY, 28th APRIL 1974   KICK-OFF 2 pm

CROWN &
MANOR F.C.
V
EX SPURS
ALL STARS XI

Entry with programme only
25p

CROWN & MANOR F.C.

GROUND

ALBURY RIDE

CHESHUNT.

SPARTAN LGE.

BOXING

Promoter
HARRY GROSSMITH

BOXING

SHOREDITCH TOWN HALL

Matchmaker: Mickey Duff   OLD STREET, E.C.1   Gen. Manager: Archie Kasler

TUESDAY, 9th MAY, 1961

Doors open 7.00 p.m.   Commence 8.00 p.m.

THE MOST CONTROVERSIAL MATCH EVER PRESENTED AT THIS HALL

8 (3 min) Rounds Feather-weight Contest at 9-2

BILLY   DANNY

DAVIS v O'BRIEN

WEST HAM   KILBURN

DONT MISS THIS THRILLING MATCH BETWEEN LONDON'S TWO
UNDEFEATED YOUNG CHAMPIONSHIP PROSPECTS

6 (3 min) Rounds Light-weight Contest at 9-12

VIC ANDREETTI v GILL NEILL

Hoxton. Another grand prospect.   Belfast. One of Britains most ex-
Just K.Od Joe Jacobs I Round   perienced boxers

6 (3 min) Rounds Light-weight Contest at 9-12

ALAN PALMER v DENNIS BROWN

Norwood. Only one defeat in 10   Leicester. Only one defeat
contests. Never fails to please.   in 6 contests

6 (3 min) Rounds Fly-weight Contest at 8-5

MICKEY TAHENY v GERRY JONES

West Ham. Brilliant ex amateur   Wigan. A good test for any boxer

6 (2 min) Rounds Light Heavy-weight Contest at 12-9

ROCKY NELSON v MICKEY MURPHY

Brixton. First Pro fight   Bury

PLUS SUPPORTING CONTEST

Tickets :   21/-   12/6   7/6   5/-   Special Ringside
42/-

Obtainable from: Archie Kasler (Ley 7044 & Bis 1775) Harry Grossmith (Cli 3911)
Shoreditch Town Hall (Sho 7600) Mickey Duff (Sta 8511) Curley's Cafe (Bis 2128)
Sid's Fruit Shop (Bis 1775)   Frank Goldberg (Tulse 6019)   Al Phillips (Can 5852)
Stan Courtney, 122, Caledon Road, E.6 (Gra 9113)   Stan Moss, 10, New Barn St,
(Alb 3816)   Les Madison, 18 Morgan Street, E.16 (Alb 1692)
Tony Mancini, "The Lord Palmerston" 648, Kings Road, Fulham (Ren 4501)

Printed by L. Verby & Sons (TU) 172 Stoke Newington Rd. N.16

previous A 1961 handbill promoting boxing matches at Shoreditch Town Hall, early in Vic Andreetti's career. *above* Inside Andreetti's café in Hoxton Street.

Professional boxing helped to supplement the boxer's income from his day job. Some bare knuckle fighters started out as boxers, but lost their license.

Fighting is often a tradition within families such as the Walls and the McLeans. Lenny McLean, 'the Guv'nor', was Hoxton born and bred and the most successful bare knuckle fighter Britain has ever produced. One of his most famous fights was against 'the King of the Gypsies'. As the referee was telling both men he wanted a good, clean fight, his opponent nutted Lenny. As Steve at Mr Samwidges told us "this was not a good move, it took eight men to hold Lenny back and he went on to win the fight." Lenny was also flown to America to take on the Mafia's champion and won that fight too. His fighting career lasted from the late 1960s to the early 1980s. Lenny lived with his family in Geffrye Court. He was the Head Doorman at the Camden Palace among other clubs. He also ran Harold's newsagent. His patience with things like adding up was limited, so if kids bought a large assortment of penny and halfpenny sweets, he'd just say "give us a bob."

There were no Queensberry Rules with bare fist fights. They were lucrative but also unlicensed, so there were highly organised fights as well as ones that just flared up at the pub, where two men would go outside and bets would be placed. This was called 'fighting on the cobbles'. Mark Brooks recalls one local boxer who made a living fighting twice a day all over London. He told Mark he was offered double money at the Queen's (Head) to fight without gloves, but this would cost more in the long run as it could leave him unable to fight for days.

Fights would take place in halls as well as in the upstairs rooms of pubs. Shoreditch Town Hall was a premier boxing venue up to its closure in the 1970s. The acoustics there were reportedly so good that a private joke told at the ringside had the whole hall laughing.

Vic Andreetti is one of Shoreditch's most famous boxers. He became the British and Empire Lightweight Champion. Betty Kemp recalled the Andreettis: "The sons went into the pub business; they had a pub in Kingsland Road. I ended up working with Rosie, a sister-in-law of the Andreettis. Her son was an electrician and they were a respectable family. The family had two cafés down Hoxton Street near Allwright's the butchers and one before St Leonards. Because they were the boxers, naughty boys hung out there. They weren't naughty to us, no one touched you. They only hurt each other."

Sylvester Mittee, who lived in Phillipp Street at the time, made good in boxing in the 1980s. Sylvester was British and Commonwealth Welterweight champion. After his career in boxing ended, he became a sports development worker in Hackney, and continued to inspire local youngsters. Other local boxers include Jason Matthews and Micheal Watson, who both trained at the Crown and Manor Club.

left Sylvester Mittee. *above* boys playing in Essex Street.

YOUNGSTERS OUT AND ABOUT

Shoreditch has many schools, and most had nicknames which change over time. The old Pitfield Boys School (now the site of the Shoreditch Spa centre) was called Pitfield Pisspots, and the girls' school was called Crondall Crumpets. A whole book could be dedicated to the experiences of the students whose adult recollections form the heart of this book. Here are a few of the memories about leisure time in and out of school.

Peggy Crowe nee Moggridge, born in 1921, recalls the infants' school in Redvers Street. The caretaker, Jack, would open the playground out of hours and let the kids play. She recalls that "You never went out without the baby of the family." This was to take the pressure off mothers whose lot of caring for large families in cramped conditions was a considerable feat of survival. Tom Carlow remembers After School Play Centres in schools, so parents could work. It cost tuppence to join. There'd be a bit of homework, some painting or metal or wood work for the older kids.

SHOREDITCH SCHOOLS
MUSICAL ASSOCIATION
1934

ANNUAL CONCERT
SHOREDITCH TOWN HALL

SIDNEY KIRBY, 13 years (Scawfell St. School)

Schools also had concerts and held dances for the children. Norma Edwards has fond memories of going to Pitfield Boys' School when she was a teenager in the 1950s for a weekly girls' evening. They had various dances, including one to a song that went 'Horsey, horsey, don't you stop, let your feet go clippity clop'.

Joyce Howes used to go to dances at Gopsall Street School. She and her partner won a jitterbug competition there. She got the cigarettes while he got the chocolates! Older girls learnt to cook, sew and iron at the school in evening sessions. Joyce also went to the Leysian Mission in City Road before the war. It had Brownie, Scout and Girl Guide groups, as well as magic lantern shows and lectures and debates for grown-ups. A canteen in the basement kept youngsters off the streets.

In the 1930s, Shoreditch Schools collectively held concerts at Shoreditch Town Hall. The cover for the 1934 programme is illustrated opposite. It was designed by 13 year old Sidney Kirby from Scawfell Street School. Every school participated in the concert and choir members were selected from them all. The programme covered many tastes, as can be seen from the 1934 offering below:

♪ *Junior Choir with eleven songs ranging from*
   The Lotus Flower by Schumann to the Cockyolly song
♪ *Percussion Band with five songs ranging from*
   Mozart to 'The Elf, the Giant and the Gnome'
♪ *Dancing display from Chatham Gardens, Hamond Square,*
   Laysterne, Shoreditch Central and Napier Street Schools
♪ *Senior Choir with eight songs ranging from*
   Mendelssohn to 'Sunbeams'
♪ *Closing hymn*

Bomb sites dotting the area provided adventure playgrounds. Two of the biggest are now Shoreditch and Haggerston Parks. The reader will find that health and safety was not a consideration for kids playing on them, and we've seen the scars to prove it! In fact, Shoreditch's Mayor in 1946 complained that youngsters had "nowhere to go except among the rubble".

above Alan Shea on his bike in Colville Estate in the late 1960s.

Sometimes that rubble offered up more than just a space to play. In 1940, a bunch of friends had become accustomed to playing in a deserted, bombed out café in Bridport Place. One of the kids was discovered by the police opening an old can of peas he found, and was arrested for looting. This child was Walter Probyn and he was only nine years old. He was the son of a cabinet maker, and one of six children. His arrest and subsequent detention was the start of a life of crime as the notorious 'Angel Face Probyn', as recorded in his autobiography 'Angel Face – the Making of a Criminal'.

Cafés provide somewhere for young and old alike to meet and hang out. Terry Briggs liked going to Ted's near Hyde Road in the 1960s. It was done up as a 1950s American diner with red vinyl seats, Formica tables, a jukebox and a pin-table. Edie Murphy remembers a similar café in Laburnum Street. The kids couldn't afford to go in, so they hung around on the corner opposite. The woman who ran it would see them there and turn up the music so the kids could dance outside.

Steve Hiscott recalls the Hoxton Café – a youth project in the 1960s based in a shop next to the Post Office in Hoxton Street where kids could listen to music and hang out. It was run by Barry, who used to get celebrities to visit. Steve recalls: "He got Stirling Moss down to meet us. He brought a brand new Mini Cooper with him. When he went inside to get a cup of tea, Barry warned him to watch the car as the kids could nick it. Stirling said there was no problem as the car had the most sophisticated locks ever known. He came out after five minutes to see the car being driven off down the road by a pair of kids. They brought it back – they just wanted to show him it could be done."

Shoreditch has some long-standing youth clubs with many activities. For example, Crown and Manor's Dramatic Society won first place in the London Federation of Boys Clubs Competition in 1941. Jimmy Doyle, Charlie Compton and Alf Camp are remembered with respect for the work they put into the club. The Lion Club was run by Dickie Pates in the 1950-60s, who was a toastmaster at Claridges for his day job. He'd get celebrities he met through work to come to the club. At Mr Samwidges, we were told: "He did a lot for local kids – he literally kept us off the streets and out of trouble."

And there have been marching bands in the area for a long time. Several people remembered them playing music round the streets. Mary Walker recalls the Boys' Brigade brass band in the streets "every Sunday with a big drum and flags" until recent times. The ATC 444 Squadron's band carries on the tradition today.

FIRE AND WATER

The Regent's Canal has always been a magnet for local people. The London Angling Club held many a competition on its murky waters. On most days, along the canal, anglers can be found passing their time, as they have done since time immemorial. The catch may well be exotic these days, as people have released pet fish, which have outgrown their bowls, into the canal and there might be the odd crayfish or terrapin.

The canal provides a prime playground for children. We heard numerous tales of swimming as well as bathing in the canal. Ted Harrison, writing about the period up to 1918, recalls using the hot water outlet pipe from a factory to bathe in. The water washed the shingle at the side of the canal clean and kids would go there, Lifebuoy soap in hand.

above Regent's Canal by Whitmore Bridge, 1950.

Ted recalls them "swimming 'half-moon' or 'full moon', depending on how much of your bottom you showed the world." A more risqué trick was to float on your back and expose one small piece of your anatomy to anyone passing by. This was called 'cock above water'. People were generally amused and threw coins at the cheeky swimmers.

Nowadays, Laburnum Boat Club, run by Jim Armstrong since the late 1980s, gives local kids safer ways to get wet.

Pat Murphy was one of the few local kids who "didn't like the look of it" and preferred to wash at Haggerston Baths. However, his father had no problem with swimming in the canal. In an act of bravery, he even jumped in to save the life of a kid who was learning to swim and not making it.

A bath at Haggerston Baths cost between a penny and sixpence. You had to take your own soap, but could call out for "more hot water". Because there were always queues, "you could have as much hot water as you wanted, but only had about 10 minutes for your bath before being turfed out." Tom Carlow's grandmother worked there, so the family got to linger longer. At the end of the day, his gran would give Tom some of the pennies which she'd got in tips.

above Shoreditch Reflections on the Regent's Canal.

Bonfire and Fireworks Night has always been a major event in Shoreditch. People recall the excitement of walking round the streets seeing bonfires and barbecues and fireworks. Both Chas Bliss in Fellows Court and Mary Tagoe in Sara Lane Court say one of the benefits of the tower block flats is that you can watch firework displays right across London.

Local youth would plan their bonfires months in advance. They were always on the look out for wood from old bomb sites and derelict houses as well as crates left from the market and pallets from factories. Wood scavenging would take place over a mile away sometimes. Leading up to Bonfire Night, storage was a problem as they didn't want their wood stolen by another gang. The Colville boys found a creative solution in the 1950s and 60s. Terry Briggs told how "We'd sink the wood (in the canal) for our bonfire to stop others nicking it." The timber was pulled out just in time to dry out for November 5th. The bonfire was built on the bomb site where Britannia Leisure Centre is now. On the east side of Kingsland Road in the 1950s, kids would use the site where Fellows Court is now, as it was a safe distance from the houses. Kids scavenged potatoes from the market and saved up to buy fireworks. The potatoes were baked on the fires until they were black – but they tasted good.

At the end of the 1970s, about forty lads built a bonfire forty to fifty feet high (being sunk in the old basements, there was another ten foot below ground too) on the corner of Hyde Road and Pitfield Street. A rival group's fifteen foot high effort in the then Colville Estate's football pitch along Hyde Road was allowed to go first. No contest – the flames, when the taller fire was lit, reached as high as Harwood Court. It was reported as the biggest bonfire in London.

right advert for Shoreditch Night at the 1951 Festival of Britain.

SHOREDITCH NIGHT OUT

…/ arrangement with His Worship the Mayor, Alderman … J. Touchard, J.P., who will attend, Shoreditch Borough Night will take place at the Gardens on:

THURSDAY, SEPTEMBER 27th

MAKE THIS NIGHT A

FESTIVAL OF FUN

DANCING	**SHOREDITCH BEAUTY CONTEST**	FOUNTAINS
TREE WALK	Guard of Honour by	MAGIC CLOCK
THEATRES	No. 444 (SHOREDITCH) SQUADRON A.T.C.	ORCHESTRAS
GROTTO	*(By Permission of the C.O. P/O. V. WHITFIELD)*	ZOO
RESTAURANTS	**Gymnastic Display by**	BEER GARDENS
MARIONETTES	**SHOREDITCH CROWN & MANOR CLUB**	PUNCH AND JUDY
ILLUMINATIONS	**MAMMOTH FUN FAIR**	MILITARY BAND

Even if I grow rich, I'll never leave Shoreditch

Shoreditch people never miss an opportunity for a celebration. Festivals, carnivals and street parties have a long tradition.

In 1901, the Merry May Day parade was led by the 6'4" tall Cartmel Robinson, the socialist parson at Holy Trinity Church. He said "I wanted to teach these youngsters that life means happiness and not merely a struggle for bread and butter." And for that day, he was successful. There were flags flying from every window, a May Queen, old England dancers and songs, a Maypole, a Jack in the Green, gypsy encampment and merry procession. People dressed up as Robin Hood and other characters in fancy costumes, sometimes made of paper, and there were smiles everywhere. Nickie Lodge remembers many May Day parades, complete with Maypole, in St John's Garden after the war.

Edie Murphy says "every year there were flags out on the estates and street parties for something". For the Coronation in 1951, the best decorations were said to be found in Essex Street which was just off Hoxton Street, north of Falkirk Street. This was infamous as one of the toughest streets in London, but they still pulled together. Edie Murphy recalls running past it every time as "you were frightened out of your life in case you got a wallop". Joyce Howes' mother-in-law's mother used to run Marnies, the greengrocers in Essex Street. Joyce agrees it was a rough street but "If you didn't have a dinner today, you'd have one tomorrow", meaning the neighbours would make sure you ate one way or another "like a Robin Hood kind of thing."

left *A float from the 1979 Shoreditch Festival carnival, Robbo at the back with Arden Estate youngsters.*

left Essex Street Party in 1944.

Every royal event had street parties galore. Endless creativity meant that those with little to spare made it an event to remember. In 1981, for the Royal Wedding, Provost Estate had bunting made from carrier bags covering the area and pictures of the royal couple framed by the windows from old washing machines. On VE day, there were parties on every street: Tom Carlow wondered where everything came from as there was furniture, party hats and food everywhere, despite the rigours of rationing.

Big carnivals returned to Shoreditch in 1958. This started off a week of celebrations, including concerts, floodlit dances in each ward and traditional entertainment such as the Yard of Ale contest. Every area in Shoreditch made its own float for the parade and everyone mucked in. All the businesses were dressed up, even the coal carts, and stall holders wore fancy hats. The cows in Hoxton Street would be on show, surrounded by balloons, with a display of milking given. There were barbecues at the top of Hoxton Street where Crispin's yard used to be. Harry Allwright roasted a pig on a spit and the programme claimed it as 'the first time a barbeque has been held in London'.

In 1979, this tradition was picked up by the Shoreditch Festival. Run by and for local people, Shoreditch Festival continued for over 10 years. Bob Walker remembers "a great sense of achievement". On the day of the first Festival, he was filled with pride that "we did this". The first chair was Rose Lowe, followed by Terry Briggs. Terry got involved when people came to the Stag looking for five-a-side football entrants for the Festival tournament. He'd seen the previous year's efforts and his remark about piss ups and breweries was met with "you do better then". And he did. Local resourcefulness was needed time and again: in 1982, there was to be an open air boxing tournament. But when Charlie Compton and Jim Ives went to get the portable boxing ring from under the stage of Shoreditch Town Hall, two days before the event, they found it was broken beyond repair. Within twenty four hours, another boxing ring was sourced, transported and erected in Shoreditch Park – all at no cost.

below St Mary's Estate float from the 1958 Shoreditch Carnival.

LION BOY'S
OLYMPICS

SHOREDITCH FESTIVAL
SHOREDITCH FESTIVAL 79
A little of
what you
fancy does
you good.

St Anne's Church Hall became the base for everything from meetings to screen printing festival T-shirts. Jim Ives, the festival organiser, set up shop there. The Treasurer was Ian Brooks, the vicar at St Anne's, who was a familiar sight along Hoxton Street and in the Stag. Unfortunately, he had to move to a church in Liverpool after he fell in love with and married a nun from the Priory.

The Festival's most memorable Carnival float was when the 'Every One a Winner' theme got translated into 'Every One a Dinner'. The float was a giant pile of chips, covered in tomato sauce with saveloys and people dressed as pickled onions and gherkins. One festival, a tug or war was planned between the beat police, the fire brigade and the army. Only the police turned up, so Terry Briggs announced over the tannoy for anyone to take on the police team. Within seconds, Terry reports 'the whole of Murray Grove turned up.'

Eddie Thomas, the much respected local beat policeman, wrote the Festival song. The first verse and chorus went as follows:

From Old Street down the New North Road
The Shoreditch totter is looking for gold
Any old iron or old linen
If you don't want it,
Then give it to him

CHORUS: Even if I grow rich, I'll never leave old Shoreditch

The Festival ran a big event every summer and Easter, and an annual Fireshow in Shoreditch Park. The Fireshows were nothing if not ambitious – one bonfire was an enormous Houses of Parliament, and there was also a pirate galleon with treasure chest. Chas Bliss remembers "it took three days to build the bonfire and three hours to burn it down. But it was worth it." At one fireshow, John Irwin was up the top of the bonfire doing the finishing touches when the kid's procession arrived early. They were carrying torches, which got thrown on the bonfire. As Terry says, John "came down like Seb Coe."

left Clockwise from top left: Lion Club's float at the 1982 Festival, revellers preparing for the Festival at Fellows Court 1979, St Mary's Estate float, 1980, Terry Briggs (right) and John Slack preparing the Festival site on Shoreditch Park, 1980.

above Shoreditch Festival Easter Bonnets around 1980.

Festival activities included swimming galas at Haggerston Baths, pub pram races, the City Directa Cup football tournament, a two day darts tournament to try and open up the long-closed Shoreditch Town Hall. The Festival decorated Hoxton Market at Christmas for several years and initiated a number of arts projects, including the decoration of Caribbean House. It produced a quarterly newspaper, Shoreditch Views.

Shoreditch Festival created the Hoxton Garden and Hoxton Trust in 1983 to provide a seven day a week community garden for local residents, many of whom have no garden of their own. David Bellamy officially opened it and unveiled, with a puff of green smoke, a gnome in his image. The gnome mysteriously went missing one time, but was returned. The anguish of the loss is recorded in this poem by Mick Walker:

Now, I really am a happy chap,
I never like to moan,
but it really did get up my nose
when someone nicked my gnome,
so if I'm sounding mad right now,
please do beg my pardon,
but I really, really miss that fellow
from that there Hoxton Garden.
He wasn't hurting no one there,
he really loved that home -
who came that day and took him away,
who nicked my fucking gnome?

above Caribbean House in Bridport Place in the mid-1980s.

Mary Tagoe remembers many happy times in Hoxton Garden. Her children could play safely there while she kept an eye on them from her flat. She particularly remembers one event in the garden. Her daughter had her face painted with rosy red cheeks – just like Dorothy in her favourite film 'The Wizard of Oz'.

above Shoreditch Festival Parade along Hoxton Street in 2007.

In 2000, Shoreditch Trust brought in a new era for the Shoreditch Festival. Every July, a full programme of events and activities takes place over a week and sometimes longer. The Festival is now established as a major event in the London arts calendar.

Quirky is as quirke was

If there is one word bandied around today that is used to sum Shoreditch up to the wider world, it is 'Quirky'. Shoreditch features in the 'Quirky Shopping Guide'. Restaurants, bars, clothes, buildings and people are often described as being quirky, meaning unusual, or just plain weird. It's a description mostly applied to newer incomers to Shoreditch, but the word may well have its 17th century origins here.

It may stretch artistic license a bit far, but both Ben Johnson, and Shakespeare, used the word at about the exact time it appeared. In Johnson's case, he described a man as knowing "every quirke within lusts laborinth." Shakespeare, in 'Much Ado about Nothing', uses it to infer wit, as in "I may chance have some odde quirkes and remnants of witte broken on me."

An original use of the word was to describe a sudden twist, turn or curve, a flourish in short. So let's finish on a flourish by thanking the sometimes lusty, always witty and endlessly generous people of Shoreditch who have helped us write what we hope is a quirky book in celebration of Shoreditch lives.

Above is a piece of Goss crested china, made in quantities around 1900-1910 as souvenirs for tourists and most often for seaside resorts. A peculiarly English product for sure, made rarer by the fact that this one celebrates Shoreditch.

Why would someone bother to produce this? Pride of course. Pride in a past well lived, pride in a shared future, pride in an area unique, special, famous, sometimes infamous but, above all, full of life.

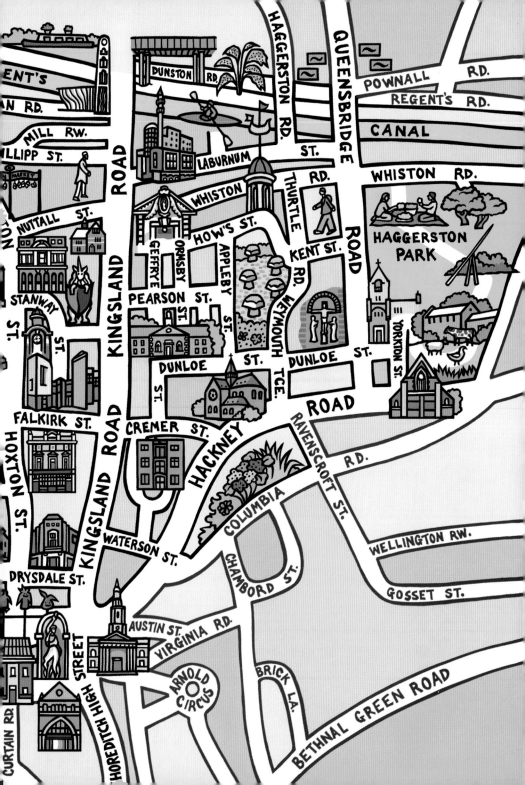

ACKNOWLEDGMENTS

Thanks

We are indebted to all those who gave their time to take part. There are many more we could have included if there was time. It is a testament to peoples' loyalty to the area that everyone we spoke to wanted to contribute. We would like to thank the following:

CONTRIBUTORS

Janie Adie, Alice, Linda Anderson, Chas Bliss, Terry Briggs, Mark Brooks, Doreen Bullock, Irene Cakebread, Tom and Val Carlow, Steve Collis, Joe Cooke, Peggy and Harry Crowe, Jo Dorking, Kathleen Doyle, Norma Edwards, Rose Heatley, Steve and Linda Hiscott, Joyce Howes, Jim Ives, Melek Kazim, Betty Kemp, Nickie Lodge, Harry Morris, Edie and Pat Murphy, Lily Nottage, Gwen Plume, John Sawyer, Alan Shea, Kay Stone, Mary Tagoe, Bob Walker, Mary Walker, Maureen Walker, Mick Walker.

And those who are no longer with us: Grace Blaketer, Harry Browne, Peggy Edwards, Ted Harrison, Maurice Lautman, Marie McCourt, Franny Sydes, George Turnell.

PHOTO CREDITS

Ken Flaherty: *4, 44, 53, 61, 73, 75, 79, 100, 123, 136, 137, 172.*
Steve Hiscott: *front cover, 147.* Hackney Archives: *2, 8, 10,
13, 14, 16, 25, 28, 30, 32, 40, 43, 48, 52, 59, 68, 70, 74, 76,
82, 83, 89, 90, 93, 97, 102, 107, 108, 115, 124, 135, 140, 142,
149, 154.* Jim Ives: *6, 50, 54, 105, 117, 162, 164.* Rob Smith:
120. London Transport Museum: *15.* Peter Haddon: *21-
23.* Hackney Gazette: *26, 95, 161.* Mark Brooks: *27, 39, 60.*
Shoreditch Trust: *34, 66, 71, 94, 166.* Carlaina Edwards:
56. George Turnell: *61.* Lily Yeomans: *63, back cover.* Alan
Shea: *116, 134, 152.* Mary Walker: *130, 138.* Peggy Crowe:
131. Elizabeth Whiter née Hunt: *132.* Unknown: *55, 80, 98,
141, 148.* Free Form Arts Trust: *155, 165.* Charlie Young: *158.*
Ron Mercer: *160.* Terry Briggs: *162.* Chas Bliss: *162.*

MAPS

Ordnance Survey: *17-18, inside front and back cover.* Hackney
Archives: *12.* Booths Poverty Map: *84-85.* Jane Smith and
Rob Smith, The Universal Map Company: *168-169.*

MEMORABILIA

Carolyn Clark: *27,57, 58, 86, 88, 110, 111, 112, 119, 126-8, 146,
150,162, 167.* Unknown: *121, 129, 156.* Norma Edwards: *38.*
Harry Morris: *144-145.*

AND

John Pulford: *Printing advisor.*
John Pulford and Lou White: *Proof reading.*

Authors

Carolyn Clark lived in Shoreditch from 1976 and moved to the Hackney Road area in 1980. She was Secretary of the Shoreditch Festival from 1979 to 1985 and edited 'Shoreditch Views' community newspaper. Carolyn was Deputy Chief Executive of Shoreditch Trust from 2000 to 2009 and wrote the Past and Present columns in 'In Shoreditch' magazine.

Linda Wilkinson is a playwright, novelist, scientist and historian. Her book 'Watercress But No Sandwiches – Three Hundred Years of the Columbia Road Area' was a winner of the Raymond Williams Prize. She lives in Bethnal Green where her family have resided for over a century.